JEAN PERRY SPODNIK
and BARBARA GIBBONS

The 35-Plus Diet
for Women

The Breakthrough Metabolism Diet
for Women Over 35

PAN BOOKS
London, Sydney and Auckland

First published in the USA 1987 by Harper and Row Publishers
First published in Great Britain 1988 by Souvenir Press Ltd
This edition published by Pan Books Ltd,
Cavaye Place, London SW10 9PG

9 8 7 6 5 4 3

© Jean Spodnik and Barbara Gibbons 1987

ISBN 0 330 30755 X

Photoset by Parker Typesetting Service, Leicester

Printed and bound in Great Britain by
Richard Clay Ltd, Bungay, Suffolk

This book is dedicated in
the memory of my mentors:
Clara Perry, my mother
Professor Helen A. Hunscher, Ph.D, R.D.
Professor Frances E. Fisher, M.S., R.D.

— Jean Perry Spodnik
Pepper Pike, Ohio
August 1986

The 35-Plus Diet For Women

Jean Perry Spodnik has had thirty years' experience in the field of dietetics. Since 1971 she has been Lead Clinical Dietician at the Kaiser Permanente Medical Center in Cleveland, Ohio, and she is also an instructor in Case Western Reserve University's Department of Nutrition. Her research into the weight problems of midlife women grew out of her attempts to deal with her own weight gain following a hysterectomy, and the success of her theory has been proved in a controlled study that showed a dramatic difference in weight loss between women using her diet and those using conventional low-calorie diets.

Barbara Gibbons writes a 'Slim Gourmet' column which is syndicated in more than 200 daily newspapers in the United States. She is the author of *The Slim Gourmet Cookbook, Lean Cuisine* and many other diet cookbooks.

Contents

ONE

The 35-Plus Diet for Women

Before starting a diet, check with your doctor to be sure it is appropriate for you to go on one, and that the diet you have selected is suitable for you.

While following the diet, if you experience any unexpected or unusual reactions or symptoms, consult your doctor promptly.

The case histories in this book are based on actual situations, but in some instances the cases are composites, and in all instances the names and identifying details about each person have been changed.

Introduction

Like lots of people predestined by genes to fatten up on fewer calories, I've found myself preoccupied by weight control, first as a frustration and finally as a career.

From the tubbiest toddler on the block, I grew to be the fattest kid in the eighth grade at 208 pounds. I spent the next twenty years exploring all the diets that don't work. In my thirties – married and a mother – I finally found slimness. Quite simply, I taught myself how to cook all over again.

Accepting finally the fact that I couldn't eat like other people, I began editing out the unnecessary calories that made favourite foods more fattening than they needed to be.

Losing Weight in the Kitchen

Lightening up on calories in the kitchen is accepted practice today, but it was quite unheard of when I began doing it. I had to invent an entire cuisine just for myself, a way of cooking that focuses on:

● Lean protein foods and bulky vegetables to satisfy the appetite.
● Lots of spices and herbs and flavour-rich ethnic ingredients to make healthy food taste good.
● The avoidance of empty-caloried fats, sugars and starches.

I lost eighty pounds and managed to keep it off. Because my true goal was to lose ninety! (Frankly, it still is.) At 128 pounds I was on the low side of the charts for my 5-foot 6-inch height, but I was still short of the model-skinny slenderness idealized in the media. So, my 'diet' became permanent by virtue of never reaching its objective.

However, since my food-lover's approach led me to the exploration of ever-more interesting and exotic ways of combining low-calorie foods into interesting meals and menus, I felt no deprivation. And my new set of food choices – lean meats, poultry, seafood, fresh fruits and vegetables, whole grains, herbs and spices – became preferred.

In 1971, I 'turned pro'. As a newspaper reporter I began sharing my ideas – in print – with others who wanted to lose weight while enjoying food. The 'Slim Gourmet' column I wrote for a local newspaper quickly became syndicated, ultimately to more than two hundred newspapers. I wrote cookbooks and low-calorie cooking features in national magazines.

As a newspaper columnist for fifteen years, with weight control as my main 'beat', I've observed the flow of fads and fashions, the shift in diet focus from anti- to pro-carbohydrate. Dieters used to eat the hamburger and throw away the bread. Ten years later, by the middle eighties, the hamburger was being thrown away. The focus was on less meat and more potatoes, more breads and pastas and other starchy fare. Once shunned, they were now favoured. The diet books on the bestseller list changed from high protein to high carbohydrate.

Readers Share Weight Problems

My three-times-weekly newspaper column puts me in touch with readers' weight problems, and the mail delivers fresh insight daily. Lately there's been a noticeable increase in what I call the eat-like-a-bird letters: complaints from people, usually women, who failed to lose weight despite ultrastrict calorie-counting. Such women fill doctors' surgeries, yet more often than not reap only dismissal of their complaints. It's easy to conclude that they are simply kidding themselves. Indeed, the dietetic journals often feature research demonstrating how inept dieters are at recalling what they had for lunch and breakfast.

This marked increase in mail from women with similar complaints seemed to be coming from women entering their prime – women in their mid-thirties, and older, who were experiencing similar frustrations with conventional weight-loss regimens. As a group, they tended to be rather well informed about current thinking on nutrition, high in self-awareness, and conscientious about their weight. It didn't seem possible that all of them were deluding themselves when they reported that conventional diets just didn't work for them anymore.

It was at this point that I had a propitious meeting – in print – with Jean Perry Spodnik, the developer of the 35-Plus Diet.

In my ongoing watch for news of interest to my diet-conscious readers, I generally search several medical, health and nutrition journals every month. That's how I came upon the article in the *Journal of the American Dietetic Association* that told about a dietician's experiments at the Kaiser Permanente Medical Center in Cleveland, relating to the problems women over thirty have losing weight on conventional diets. It talked about a revolutionary diet that was achieving unprecedented success.

The three-phase diet worked its magic by precisely manipulating the *balance* among the three food elements, proteins, carbohydrate and fats, replacing simple carbohydrate foods – sugars and refined starches – with fibre-rich whole grains, fruits and vegetables. The diet augments these foods with lean protein from meat, poultry, fish and dairy products.

The intentionally nonsensational language of the medical journal masked the excitement that this diet was ultimately to cause.

For one thing, it flew in the face of the current pro-carbohydrate diet wisdom: that less meat and more potatoes are just what the doctor ordered. The spectacular success of dieters in Jean Spodnik's programme indicated that less meat and more potatoes are *not* what the doctor should order. At least not for women who are overweight and over thirty-five!

While this diet was drastically different from the high-protein fad diets of the sixties and seventies – dramatic and substantial differences we'll detail later – certain essential aspects of this diet explain why those diets were popular. The reason high-protein crash diets have always been popular is because they work – in the short run at least – and nothing succeeds like success. They work because they cause a dramatic loss of water weight in the beginning, and this is a significant morale booster.

However, they did not work in the long run, because ultimately, calories do count! Despite the fact that these high-protein fad diets provided a temporary quick fix for the water-retention aspect of women's weight problems, most of them were too high in calories and fat — animal fats in particular. Beyond that, they were woefully and often dangerously unbalanced, and uniquely dangerous to women over thirty-five. This was true for several reasons:

● The high-protein fad diets often made no distinction among the various kinds of carbohydrate. To a woman practising carbo-counting, there was little difference between chilli beans and chocolate bars. In her zeal to control the intake of carbs, it was logical to avoid the complex carbohydrates along with the simple — the whole grains, fruits and vegetables along with sugary biscuits and fizzy drinks. Constipation often accompanied these diets, but that was the least of the woes they could cause.
● High-protein diets promoted high-fat intake, which is related to increased cancer risk. And they promoted it among the very people most at risk: overweight women.
● The excessive intake of fat, especially cholesterol-laden animal fat, increases the risk of heart disease at the very age when women are beginning to lose the hormonal protection that makes them less susceptible than men.
● The often excessive and unbalanced meat intake promoted the loss of calcium from the bones — the actual washing away of bone tissue that would ultimately result in osteoporosis ('porous bones'). Tragically the person most attracted to dieting was the very person most at risk: the weight-conscious woman aged thirty-five-plus.

In the decade that followed the heyday of the best-selling high protein 'doctor diets', dieticians made their voices heard, and the dangers of these unbalanced diets became so well publicized that their appeal languished.

We Are Changing the Way We Eat

In the last ten years there have been a number of factors that worked in concert to make profound changes in our way of eating.

In the past the subject of food and cooking was primarily the preserve of housewives on the one hand and professional chefs on the other. And health? That was the preserve of the medical professional. Who wanted to hear about ailments when they sat down at the dinner table!

But now things were changing: members of youthquake had grown up. Better educated, inquisitive, iconoclastic, a new generation of adult consumer-oriented activists was moving into the mainstream. And they brought with them their dislike of plastic foods, their distrust of food manufacturers and their disinclination to hand over control of their health to doctors and drugs.

In the new era people were encouraged to take charge of their medical well-being by adopting life-style changes that would promote longevity. And everyone was urged to participate, men as well as women. Dinner was no longer disconnected from how you felt, what you weighed, how long and how well you were likely to live.

And dinner was no longer the exclusive charge of 'housewives' – since there were fewer of them.

With the soaring divorce rate and delayed marriages, many men were forced to cook for themselves. With different attitudes and the breakdown of traditional roles, many men were cooking for their families, or for the fun of it, or with health concerns in mind (and more often, all of the above). The physical fitness boom was an integral part of these changes.

The Fitness Phenomenon

The weight-control diets of the late seventies and early eighties reflected all these changes as well as the changing demographics.

Whereas in the past the typical dieter was a woman approaching, in, or past midlife (only women worried about weight gain, and this was a problem related to getting older), the more recent food and diet focus was now on body-conscious young adults, male and female, who jogged and worked out, often at the posh, upscale co-ed 'fitness centres' that were replacing singles bars. The menus that became popular mirrored the nutritional needs and life style of young, active men and women in their twenties. Red meat became a nutritional no-no, and pasta was king. Running shoes became status symbols, and marathon mania was the nation's latest sweaty excess. Laurel-crowned contenders were photographed downing plates of pasta − carbohydrate-loading − to pack in that extra energy to go the distance. A nation of headline readers got the message that starch was in.

Today, the first of a whole generation of bread-eating, pasta-loving females is beginning to push forty. Most of them do not run in marathons.

They are experiencing the thirty-five-plus weight gain double-whammy: metabolic slow down calling for fewer calories, and hormonal changes calling for tighter control of carbohydrate intake. While most of today's weight-loss diets control calories, they tend to be high in carbohydrates. *They fail to address the hormonal changes that make this group of women fail on such diets.*

All of these observations were on my mind when I read of Jean Perry Spodnik's exciting experiments. I tracked the dietician down at the Kaiser Permanente Medical Center in Cleveland and set up an interview.

An attractive, personable and compassionate woman, Jean Perry Spodnik was at first somewhat bemused by all the fuss her landmark research was creating. Her main interest was to help the ever-increasing stream of women over thirty-five who just weren't getting anywhere with weight loss by conventional means.

What I learned in researching my newspaper article was that the dietician at Kaiser Permanente Medical Center had succeeded in developing a carbohydrate-controlled diet, specifically for thirty-five-plus women, that allayed appetite and resulted in dramatic weight loss. Moreover, she had demonstrated that her unique combination of food elements worked better than conventional low calorie diets. Her dieters lost *forty per cent more weight* than a matched group of women on a conventional diet with the same number of calories.

Jean and I developed a quick rapport. I had been favourably impressed with her work in the professional journals. She had an equal admiration for my work with food, and had been bringing my books and recipes to her patients' attention. We quickly agreed to work together in bringing this diet to a wider audience, with expanded menus and a complete cookbook section with recipes designed especially for the 35-Plus Diet. We agreed that in addition to providing the diet and the recipes, we wanted also to produce a book that spoke directly to the 35-Plus Woman about the metabolic and hormonal changes that are happening to her so she understands the problems she is having and the solutions.

After this introduction, I'll turn you over to Jean for an explanation of the diet and guidance through its phases. In the second half of the book, we'll meet again through my recipes, designed specifically to bring enjoyment to the 35-Plus Diet.

BARBARA GIBBONS
Verona, New Jersey
August 1986

ONE

35 and Over: Why Nothing Seems to Work Any More

Deirdre Parker, one of my patients, has just turned forty. This puts her among America's first Yuppies. I'm sure she qualifies. She has a BMW, a PC, a VCR, an IRA and a CPA — and twenty-five pounds of excess weight she can't seem to get rid of no matter what she does! And that includes state-of-the-art exercise equipment, a semi-vegetarian diet and spa cuisine.

Cool and self-assured despite the trace of annoyance that creased her brow, Deirdre was a financial adviser, and Job One was to inspire client confidence.

'I hate to fail at things, but this weight problem has me beat. I have a closetful of expensive custom-tailored suits, and this is the only one that still fits!' It was a flawlessly tailored soft-rose tweed, set off with a pink silk shirt and a rope of pearls that were almost certainly real.

Deirdre approached her weight problem the same way she approached everything else in her life – as a challenge to be met. First there was research, books and articles to read. An intelligent, informed consumer and nobody's fool, Deirdre easily and quickly separated fad from fact. So she had decided on a diet devised from contemporary nutritional wisdom: less protein and fat, and more 'complex carbohydrates'. In other words, less meat and more potatoes. Or in Deirdre's case, less pâté and more pasta salad.

But after two weeks of dieting, Deirdre was still at ground zero, having regained in the second week the single pound she lost in the first.

Disappointed but not yet defeated, she focused on calorie counts. 'I figured it was like a company that didn't have a tight rein on costs. Slippage was somewhere, and I was determined to plug up the leaks.' She ordered the comprehensive *Composition of Foods, Handbook 8* from the Government Printing Office and began meticulous calorie book-keeping of her daily diet on a spread sheet she set up on her computer. She used a postage scale to weigh portions.

At the end of another month, Deirdre had lost three pounds on what she knew to be a 1,200-calorie, nutritionally balanced diet. On her fortieth birthday Deirdre celebrated with two scoops of Häagen-Dazs chocolate ice-cream and gained it all back.

Deirdre's experience typifies the irksome refusal of the human body to conform and perform according to predictable formulas. There's something so official and numerical about calorie guides that it's easy to slip into the expectation that our bodies will act like credit cards or bank accounts.

'I went on a semi-starvation diet for one week and the scales in the doctor's office showed a two pound weight gain. He didn't believe me and accused me of cheating.'

Such stories are nearly universal. The women who consult their doctors tend to share a common experience: an unremitting pile-up of pounds that begins in mid-thirties and escalates into midlife no matter what deprivations are undertaken to counteract it. And the doctors (usually male) don't believe them.

If you're a woman approaching or well into midlife, the chances are you're battling against weight gain. Suddenly (in some cases, or insidiously in others) the pounds pile up. What makes it all the more frustrating is that there's no dearth of diet advice. Yet the diets that seem to work for others – for your daughters, for the twenty-five-year-olds in the office, for the man in your life – just don't work for you.

You may have gone on a diet with your husband, perhaps even made a contest out of it, and in a short time he's lost the weight he wanted to lose – while you're still struggling with the first three pounds. You may have discovered that your first trip abroad – all that French and Italian food – put ten pounds on you and a month of dieting back home has lowered your spirits, but not your weight. As we leave youth behind, more and more we find that we just can't lose weight as easily as we once did. What has been a cinch becomes a challenge, then a chore, and finally an insurmountable obstacle. We may lose half a pound and then put it back on immediately – for no apparent reason.

I have been a registered dietician for thirty years and have heard these stories repeatedly from my women patients. I understand the women who come to me about weight problems at the Kaiser Permanente Medical Center in Cleveland, and I know they're telling the truth. I understand their frustration, particularly with those male diet doctors who dismiss them as cheaters and gluttons.

I have my own first-hand insight into how hormones can work mischief with the metabolism. The surgical removal of my ovaries – a hysterectomy – plunged me suddenly and prematurely into menopause. As the scale climbed incomprehensibly, I could understand the feelings of helplessness my patients were talking about.

My feelings of helplessness were all the more profound because I had all the answers – but the answers didn't work. I knew how to count calories, but somehow counting calories didn't seem to work any more. Nor did any of the other remedies: more exercise, less salt, more meals, smaller servings. I found myself standing on the scale and cursing it as if it were a living, breathing thing, just as I had seen so many of my patients do in helpless frustration after a week of white-knuckled table-pushing yielded no loss whatsoever.

I didn't know what was happening, but I did have an idea, and I sought federal funding to test a theory I had. The shared experience of my over-thirty-five Kaiser Permanente dieters seemed to suggest that as women proceed into their prime, there are subtle but profound changes in metabolism that are out of sync with today's eating fashions.

The Prime-of-Life Water Problem

The core of the problem seems to be secret water retention, leading to a fat and fluid build-up that signals its presence mainly on the scales. Or in swollen hands and feet. Take the case of Alice, a recent divorcee.

Alice had intended to make a grand gesture: pulling the wedding ring off her finger and tossing it at her ex's feet, just as he had tossed away her and their twenty-three-year marriage. But the actual scene was almost comic: the gold band refused to come off – it was wedged between two ridges of puffy, translucent flesh. Alice's fingers were always like that at night. If I ever get a chance to replay this scene, Alice told herself grimly, I'll do it in the morning. She still had her sense of humour.

Scientific studies have shown that, after thirty-five, women are plagued with a special kind of fluid retention. My research revealed that this wasn't the ordinary pound or two you add temporarily during a heat wave or after an excessively salty meal.

I'm not talking about pre-period puffiness, either. Significant premenstrual bloat usually starts in our thirties and is much worse for some than for others. Each month, before our periods begin, our bodies produce fewer hormones, and this deficiency will cause fluid retention and premenstrual tension. (It also raises insulin levels, by the way, which in turn causes hunger, particularly the craving for sweets that many of us experience right before our periods are due. But that's another story we'll get into later.)

I'm talking here about a phenomenon common to many women in their thirties, forties and fifties. Conventional calorie counting is no match for the problem. Sodium-restriction diets fail to work in the long run. Moreover, the current switch to high-carb diets, low in meat, appears to be all wrong for many midlife women. However healthy they are for men and for younger women, for women in midlife they can contribute to water retention and bloating.

After thirty-five, as we move closer to what the doctors call premenopause, we have a diminishing production of all female hormones with each menstrual cycle. And the hormone production does not increase after the period is over, as it did when we were younger.

The human body is composed of a significant amount of water. How is the water distributed in our bodies? Ideally, about half of it is inside the cells, and the rest of it is outside, between the cells and in the blood.

Here again, however, men and women differ. And fat people and thin people differ. Lean individuals with lots of muscles and little fat tend to have more of their body water within the cells. Women, especially fat women, tend to have more water between the cells.

When we retain water, it flows from the blood to the spaces between the cells, and the result is puffiness: thickened waistlines and bloated bellies. For some, but not all, it may also cause more obvious swelling in the legs and arms, especially the hands.

What's happening?

Our kidneys are performing an over-enthusiastic favour for our blood. Since the blood must have sodium (salt) to do its job, the kidneys hold on to sodium so that blood is assured of an adequate supply. However, in the case of the bloated woman, the kidneys are storing too much sodium. And the body responds by matching the oversupply of sodium with an over-balance of water between the cells. The result? You can't get your shoes on or your ring off. Belts and blouses may not fit any more, either!

Get rid of extra sodium your body is retaining, and you'll get rid of the excess fluid between the cells.

The logical remedy, you would think, is to go on a low-sodium diet and attempt to eliminate visible salt from your diet. I say visible, because you can't eliminate the natural sodium in the food itself. For a low-sodium diet to help this kind of water retention, you would have to reduce sodium intake to less than one gram. That's tough, believe me! It's one of the most unpalatable diets there is – and very difficult to manage, requiring all sorts of special products. Since sodium is vital to life, such a diet is not without dangers also. You'd need to be under a doctor's care if you were going to restrict your sodium intake that drastically.

You might also get your physician to prescribe a diuretic (water pill). But prolonged use of diuretics without strict supervision may cause kidney damage. (Did you know that some reducing pills purchased over the counter actually contain a diuretic: ammonium chloride? You should be wary of using such preparations without medical advice.)

Neither diuretics nor salt-free diets have proved to be much help with the kind of weight problem that plagues the thirty-five-plus woman.

A Quick Fix for Water Weight

However, there is a kind of diet that does provide a quick fix for water-weight problems. Promoters of fad diets have known about it for years. I call it the 'Get Rich Quick Diet' because it has helped line the pockets and fund the retirement accounts of lots of diet promoters – without really solving the weight problems. Women may lose ten or fifteen pounds (more accurately, pints) very quickly and rave to their friends about this kind of diet, thereby helping to promote sign-ups or sales. But the minute they go off the diet, the body compensates and quickly brings its store of water back to pre-diet levels.

It is the high-protein fad diet, and variations on it move in and out of fashion like shoulder pads and skirt lengths. It's been around for more than a hundred years in one form or another. And it's not only hucksters who employ this kind of diet. Variations of it are also used by concerned and ethical physicians who are trying desperately to help their overweight patients slim down. They use it because they know it works. But they don't know why. Or even with whom. They couldn't quite account for its effectiveness because until now there was no scientific evidence to back it up. But experience (what the medical community calls 'anecdotal evidence') taught them that it worked more often than other methods. Why did it work? Chances are, most of their patients were 35-Plus Women. The majority of dieters have always been women over thirty-five, the patients most likely to show dramatic weight losses on a short-term high-protein, low-carbohydrate regimen.

The Ketogenic Diet Extreme

Most of the fad diets over the years delivered initial quick water-weight loss by taking the high-protein diet to an extreme – by putting the dieter into ketosis.

Ketosis is a complication of starvation, a condition that results from the incomplete combustion of fatty acids. It's an outcome of following a diet with too little food, or more specifically, too few carbohydrates. While ketosis is a condition most would normally want to avoid, some of the high-protein fad diets purposely brought it about by recommending diets devoid of adequate carbohydrate. Foods are composed primarily of protein, fat and/or carbohydrate in various combinations. By manipulating the diet to short-change basic carbohydrate needs – by minimizing not only sugars and starches but also fruit, grains, legumes and vegetables – the body could be thrown into ketosis even though caloric intake in the form of protein and fat was adequate.

But ketosis is dangerous. The US Council on Foods and Nutrition published a statement criticizing these high-protein, high-fat diets. They warned of metabolic problems that could develop as a result. These problems are related to the excessive excretory demands of the high-protein intake and included the possibility of life-threatening electrolyte imbalance. With most of these diets, the dieter is directed to stay on them for only a very short time (usually no more than two weeks), because the authors are aware of their harmful effects.

In fact, many of these high-protein diets allow unlimited amounts of high-fat foods and ultimately don't result in weight loss at all. If your energy (calorie) intake is greater than your output (calorie needs), there is no way that you can lose weight. You may lose excessive water, but not actual fat. And once you stop dieting, the water comes back.

The hormonal mischief that causes women to suffer fluid retention is only one of the factors that makes weight loss a bigger challenge for women than for men. The average woman is programmed from puberty onwards to store more fat than her male counterpart does.

Female Metabolism

Let me tell you about one of my patients, Maggie. When I first met her, she was visibly shaking with outrage – over a word. The word was 'obese'.

That's what Maggie's doctor had written down on her medical record. She had come to see him about her tiredness. When he left her alone in the examining room, Maggie tentatively tipped open the folder to see what he had written. And there was that word.

'What an awful word,' Maggie wailed. Her doctor had referred her to me. I had the feeling that the text of her medical record was going to take precedence over losing weight. If I could have reclassified her as 'big-boned' or even 'substantially proportioned', she might have gone home in peace. But 'obese'?

Having gained thirty-five pounds since college, Maggie would have grudgingly owned up to being perhaps a bit 'overweight'. But 'obese' brought to mind 'circus fat ladies, forgodsakes!'

But overweight and obese are not the same.

Obesity is the medical term for excessive fatness. To take Maggie's circus example, the strong man is 'overweight'. With his mantle of muscle, he weighs more than the average man of his height – even though he is actually underfat. But the circus fat lady (and Maggie, too, but I'm not going to tell her) are 'overfat'. In a word, obese.

It's probably safe to conclude that any woman who is thirty or more pounds heavier than the average woman of the same height is obese.

Why is it that the prime of life is marred for so many women by a relentless battle with the scales? Why is it that, for many of us, maturity brings obesity? The answer lies in our basic hormonal and metabolic make-up.

Metabolic Mischief

'My metabolism is low.'

That's not simply an excuse used by lazy gluttons to explain away excess pounds. It is *the* reason why some people – especially women approaching midlife – start turning food into fat instead of fuel. Coupled with increased water retention, it spells double trouble for women over thirty-five.

But why is your metabolism low? Why now and not before? Why you and not him? Why do you feel like the fat lady married to the strong man? Too much food for you is never enough for him.

What is metabolism? *Metabolism* is a general term used to cover all the chemical changes that go on in the tissues of the body.

The 'basal metabolic rate' – your BMR – represents the irreducible minimum of energy required to keep up the life process, the internal work of the body. It is usually defined as the minimum amount of energy required by the body – the absolute least you would need when lying at rest in a comfortable environment, neither too hot nor too cold, completely relaxed, twelve to fifteen hours after the last meal. (Even digestion takes some energy.) You say that if you hadn't eaten for fifteen hours, you'd be anything but relaxed? Well, this is the theoretical 'bottom line' that helps measure your basic energy needs. The energy used to fuel the body can be measured: another term for a measure of energy is calorie. Unfortunately for the fat lady, pound for pound it takes *fewer* calories to maintain her weight than it does for the strong man to maintain his, because fat takes very little energy to maintain.

Studies have shown that grossly obese people tend to be relatively inactive. While the movements they do make are expensive in calories, they move so much less than people of average weight that their stores of excess fat run little risk of being diminished.

But what many people do not realize is that muscles are *never* completely relaxed. Muscular tone is necessary even in sleep. Therefore, the muscular person will burn more calories, *even at rest*, than the obese person.

What does this mean for our extreme examples, the circus fat lady who is overfat and the circus strong man who is over-muscled? Simple. If they both tipped the scale at the same weight, the strong man could lose weight on a diet that would make the fat lady gain.

Hormones

You may be wondering why, in this era of equal opportunities, circuses still continue to feature strong *men* and fat *ladies*. To be sure, there are a lot more female body builders around today, but rarely do they achieve the spectacular musculature that their male counterparts do. Male hormones lead to the development of more muscles. Women's hormones, on the other hand, lead to the storage of fat. It's as simple as that.

Hormones dictate the laying down of fat on the female body in preparation for child-bearing. From the very beginning of time, female physiology has been geared towards storing fuel in preparation for reproduction. When humans were hunters and gatherers, women had to be prepared not to gather while carrying their young. As soon as the young female of our species reaches puberty, her shape changes, and she begins to accumulate some fat around the hips. This accelerates during actual pregnancy. In the fourth to the sixth month even naturally slender women start to store fat around the derrière. I explain this to my young expectant mothers: nature arranges things so that you can live off your own fat while the baby-to-be lives off your food.

Because of different body compositions in males and females, men have more active tissue than women. As little girls mature into young women, their hormones favour fat storage. As women mature and experience further hormonal changes, body composition continues to change: to less active tissue and more fat.

I use the term 'active tissue' to describe men's muscles and 'less active tissue' to describe fat. Actually, fat is just about inert. Think of it as simple *storage* of unused energy. Like anything tucked away unused and unneeded, it requires virtually no maintenance. The cost of its upkeep is very small compared to muscle.

Here's the metabolic bottom line: because of our different body composition – men with more muscles and women with more fat – women start off with a basal metabolic rate ten per cent lower than men.

So there you have it. Nature wants you to be fa⁺¹

Actually, when Mother Nature designed metabolisms, she didn't consider modern life style, modern medicine or your modern desire to live actively into your seventies and beyond. Nor did she imagine that mothers would want to look like their teenage daughters and that grandmothers would go on honeymoons.

But wait, it gets worse! Biologically, both men and women would reach their physical peak at the age of twenty-five. Metabolically speaking, after twenty-five it's downhill all the way. For both sexes. Our basal metabolic rate starts to decrease about 0.5 per cent to 1 per cent a year, varying from individual to individual. We usually don't notice this until we are in our thirties. By our forties, there's no doubt about it: we aren't burning calories the way we used to. The fact is, more women in this age group have a basal metabolic rate of 1,000 calories or less.

How Active Are You?

In addition to your basal metabolic requirements, you must also take into account your activity level and how that affects the number of calories you need to maintain your weight. Here is a quick rule of thumb to see if you are as active as you think you are:

Very Light Activity   Sitting most of the day: reading, talking, watching TV, studying. Only two hours or less spent walking or standing. This small amount of activity would take you only 30 per cent above your basal metabolic needs. In other words, if your BMR is 1,000 calories, you would need only 1,300 calories to maintain your present weight, and anything above that would cause you to gain. Not very much, is it?

Light Exercise   Sitting, typing, standing, laboratory work, some walking. This would be 50 per cent above the BMR. It would take only 1,500 calories to maintain present weight.

Moderate Exercise   Standing, walking, housework, gardening, carpentry, etc., little sitting. This would be 70 per cent above your BMR or 1,700 calories to maintain present weight.

Strenuous Exercise   Much of the time spent actively: standing, walking, skating, outdoor games, dancing, little sitting. This would be 100 per cent above your BMR or 2,000 calories to maintain present weight.

Severe Exercise   Labourers or professional athletes – tennis, swimming, basketball, football, running, heavy work. This could be 200 per cent of your BMR or 3,000 calories to maintain present weight.

TWO

The Challenge: Finding Out What Does Work

The challenge in developing a diet for the woman over thirty-five was to put together an eating plan that would restrict excess calories but still be appealing, satisfying and nutritionally sound. At the same time, it had to get rid of the excess water and sodium in the body so that steady weight loss could take place.

Above all, it had to be a diet you could live with. A diet that leaves you hungry or edgy, that drains energy or compromises health, or one that's too demanding in what it requires or prohibits, will soon be abandoned.

A tall order!

The answer lay in food chemistry, in carefully calculating an exact balance of carbohydrate, fat and protein in the diet. To achieve maximum results **it is essential that you follow the diet exactly.** While the 35-Plus Diet is very flexible within each food category, of necessity it is very rigid in its ratios.

This diet is *not* ketogenic. You will not experience the dry-mouth, bad-taste, bad-breath symptoms so familiar with ketogenic crash diets, nor the moodiness and lack of energy — that bone-tired weariness that starts to show up after the first week of a ketogenic diet. But it still lets the 35-Plus Woman get rid of water weight without the aid of drugs. And without eliminating salt. (The salt-free diet is one of the most difficult regimens a dietician has to deal with in therapy. Compliance is very low.)

Changing Your Body Chemistry

The 35-Plus Diet is set up in three phases. The first phase actually changes your body chemistry — alters your blood's chemical composition — so that you shed excess water. The second phase lets you continue to lose fat and excess water on a balanced-for-women diet that's easy to stay on. The third phase aims at keeping the weight off for good.

Phase One   of the 35-Plus Diet is set up to bring you to the brink of ketosis, close to ketosis but not actually in it. In Phase One the composition of the diet is 27 per cent carbohydrate, 40 per cent protein and 33 per cent fat, a total of 900 calories. During this stage — which lasts one to two weeks — you can expect to lose 4 to 8 pounds.

Phase Two   of the 35-Plus Diet is 37 per cent carbohydrate, 34 per cent protein, and 29 per cent fat, a total of 950 calories. This ratio has proved to be ideal for the 35-Plus Woman Dieter, and she can stay on it as long as she needs to. Despite its low-calorie total, it's designed to be appetite satisfying, with lots of bulky fibre foods and lean protein. Unlike other reducing diets, it does not foster the frustrating water weight fluctuations that defeat women dieters.

Phase Three   is a 'soft landing' readjustment into living the rest of your life without gaining excessive water or fat. In the last phase you gradually increase the use of carbohydrate foods experimentally — with weekends off your diet or alternate days off — until you find your own safe balance.

Calories Count But You Don't Have to Count Them

On the 35-Plus Diet, calories *do* count. But you don't have to, if you follow the diet plan. The caloric level is set close to most women's basic metabolic rate after thirty-five: under 1,000 calories in a 24-hour period. You don't need to count grams of carbohydrate or protein either. If you follow the diet, you will be assured of keeping your calorie intake low enough to lose fat. And your protein, fat and carbohydrate intake will be properly balanced.

The diet has a double objective: firstly to lose fat; and secondly to force the body to give up the excessive sodium naturally, so you lose water. Keep in mind that it is the excess sodium in the body that is holding the excess water, which in turn accounts for your water-retention problems and failure to lose weight on conventional low-calorie diets.

Flushing Away Excess Water

The body normally uses carbohydrate for energy. When the diet is manipulated – when protein foods rather than carbohydrate foods are being used to supply energy – the protein breaks down into hydrogen, carbon, oxygen and nitrogen.

This last element is particularly significant. When nitrogen leaves the body by way of the kidneys, it picks up and flushes out sodium from the plasma (and potassium as well – more about that later). The body immediately seeks to replenish sodium in the plasma by taking it from the sodium-laden water between the cells – eliminating the excess water in the process.

These are the principles this diet puts to work:

● Carbohydrates yield no ketogenic bodies and are, in fact, 100 per cent antiketogenic.
● Protein yields 46 per cent ketogenic bodies and is 54 per cent antiketogenic.
● Fats yields 90 per cent ketogenic bodies and are 10 per cent antiketogenic.

All this means is that carbohydrate foods, like sugar and starch, do not promote ketosis, while protein and fat do.

Phase One of the 35-Plus Diet brings you just to the brink of ketosis by using a ratio of 1 to 1 between ketogenic and antiketogenic elements – more protein, less carbohydrate. Protein is the key here. Although fat is also on the ketogenic side of the balance, it has more than double the calories of protein, so intake of fat must be limited on a weight-loss diet. You do want to lose fat as well as water!

The careful balance of these three food elements is the key to the success of the 35-Plus Diet. While complex carbohydrates have an essential role in the diet, carbohydrate in the form of sugar is another story.

Sugar, Insulin and the Menstrual Cycle

The pernicious role of sugar in the adult woman's diet can hardly be overstressed. Sugar conspires with the interplay of women's hormones in ways that increase hunger and contribute to the laying down of fat and the retention of water between the cells.

You may have noticed an increase in sweet cravings just before your period. This is due to a drop in oestrogen that precedes the menstrual cycle. This, in turn, kicks off a whole relay of powerful hormonal recalibrations and reactions that literally turn your body into a fat-making machine:

- The decrease in oestrogen causes the pituitary gland to pump out a natural antidiuretic.
- That interferes with the body's ability to flush away salt and water – so you have water retention.
- At the same time the insulin level goes up.
- This causes hunger, particularly a craving for sweets.
- If you answer that craving with sugar and excess calories, you add to your fat stores and intensify your fluid retention problems.

Even worse, giving in to a craving for sweets sets up a self-perpetuating roller coaster ride for your blood-sugar level: sugar, especially refined sugar (sucrose), is pure carbohydrate, absorbed into the bloodstream much more quickly than any other food component. When sweet freaks and sugar junkies talk about 'mainlining' sugar, they don't know how apt the metaphor is. After eating sweets, the level of sugar in the blood skyrockets. The body answers with a rush of insulin, sending blood-sugar levels down precipitously low and setting up another bout of nervous, shaky sweet-craving – until your next sugar 'fix'.

Many women with weight and water-retention problems are on a constant sugar high. This is why many women who understand the problems they are having come to view sugar as *addictive*. It's not addictive in quite the same way that drugs are addictive, but it may be hard to tell the difference when you're on the roller coaster and your moods and energy levels peak and plummet along with your blood-sugar levels.

Happily, you can get off sugar pretty easily, simply by manipulating the diet to keep your blood-sugar levels on a fairly smooth line, rather than up and down. *You may experience sugar withdrawal during the first twenty-four to forty-eight hours of the diet.* But it will pass. The trick is to prevent the craving for sweets by filling up on lean protein and high-fibre foods. Lean protein foods (lean meat, fish, poultry, low-fat cheeses) are more slowly digested than carbohydrates. Bulky foods that are naturally high in fibre such as whole grains, vegetables and fruits – even though these contain natural fruit sugars – also slow down digestion. This promotes a flatter blood sugar response than the roller coaster ride you've been experiencing.

In dealing with this problem, you need to remember that it's not just the sweets you eat that can contribute to blood-sugar bounce. What about the sweets you drink? Sugar-sweetened soda, coffee and tea, for example. I've had patients who were doing twelve Cokes a day. Caffeine, usually found in all three, by itself lowers blood-sugar levels, making sugar withdrawal even more precipitous. If you are having problems with sugar, you should avoid these drinks or switch to sugar-free, decaffeinated brands. You should be able to tolerate moderate caffeine use again after blood-sugar levels have stabilized.

Understanding how this diet works also makes it clear why sugar rather than salt is the bloat-causing culprit for many 35-Plus Women with weight problems. It has been well established in nutrition that placing obese patients on a diet consisting totally of carbohydrates – regardless of the amount of sodium (salt) in the diet – prevents the loss of excessive sodium and water in the urine. When the same patients are then put on a diet solely of protein and fat (a ketogenic diet), they lose the sodium and water in the urine – regardless of the amount of sodium in the diet.

All of this should make it clear why it's important to be diligent in avoiding refined sugar and sugar-containing foods while following the diet. Unless you are on a sodium-restricted diet prescribed by your physician, you should follow the latest American Heart Association guidelines on salt, which suggests that you not exceed the equivalent of one teaspoon per day.

Putting the 35-Plus Diet to the Test

Like Dr Jekyll, I found my best first subject right in the mirror. It was a mirror I was starting to avoid since a hysterectomy had thrown me into 'instant menopause'.

Menopause marks the end of a woman's childbearing years but by no means the end of her vitality and sexuality. While motherhood is an important and fulfilling role, it's not the only one. The end of the childbearing cycle, coming at a time when most women would no longer want children anyway, ought to be welcomed with the same eagerness that young girls show for the beginning of the childbearing cycle.

After the ovaries are removed and a woman no longer has periods, the hormonal output ceases abruptly, not in the natural, gradual manner that usually occurs over a two-decade cycle. The forces that conspire to put on weight and water can suddenly overwhelm a woman after such surgery. I put on twenty pounds in just a few months. And not twenty pounds I could hide, either. I was bloated, distorted, and downright miserable. I love my work, and I love dealing with people, but who's going to take dietary advice from a dietician who looks like she needs to go on a diet? I remember thinking that I'd have to give up my practice and hide in the lab with a loose, white, lab coat for a uniform.

In my first week on the experimental diet I lost five pounds. It was hard not to be thrilled, even though I knew, better than anybody, that this was 'water weight', and celebration would be premature. The important questions were whether I'd continue to lose weight and if it would *stay* off. It took another two months to lose the remaining pounds. It was tempting – in view of today's extremely lean role models – to continue on and attempt to be model-slim, but my common sense and my nutrition education told me otherwise. Unreasonable expectations are a major cause of diet failure.

With my own success, I began using the diet with some of my more discouraging cases, the women who'd lose four pounds one week and gain back five the next.

What a revelation! Every last one succeeded in shedding the pounds that before had stuck to them like glue. For many of them it was their first success ever, despite years of struggle. As I began using the diet with more and more women, I knew I was on to something. What was needed now was proof that it worked better than conventional diets. Simply adding up the pounds or the people who lost weight was not enough. We needed a controlled study.

As I suspected, given the results of the first early trials, there was no lack of volunteers willing to try out any diet that even *hinted* it might solve the problems of midlife weight loss. But proper research techniques required that we have a control group for purposes of comparison. That meant that for every woman on this 35-Plus Diet, there had to be another woman – similar in age and weight – on a conventional low-calorie diet.

The research was conducted with twenty healthy women between the ages of forty and sixty who were twenty to fifty pounds overweight. Ten were put on the diet I had devised, the test diet, and the other ten served as controls. They were put on a conventional, balanced, weight-reduction diet of the same number of calories: 950. The composition of the other diet, the conventional calorie-counting diet, was 50 per cent carbohydrate, 20 per cent protein and 30 per cent fat, in accordance with the Recommended Dietary Goals for the United States set by the Select Committee on Nutrition and Human Needs of the United States Senate in 1977.

The study lasted seven weeks. Here's what happened: the

women on the conventional, control diet experienced weight fluctuations and a widely diverse range of results. Over the seven-week period they ranged from a *gain* of one and one-quarter pounds to a loss of nine and one-quarter pounds. The average weight loss for the conventional diet was three and six-tenths pounds.

Those on the 35-Plus Diet, on the other hand, experienced a steady decline in weight and lost between nine and sixteen pounds over the seven-week period. Their average loss was eleven pounds – three times the average loss of the control group.

The success of the diet over the long haul is perhaps even more significant than these figures. Dieting statistics tell us that only one person in twenty succeeds in reaching weight-loss goals and keeping weight off. But since that first experiment, we've seen steadily mounting evidence that the 35-Plus Diet gives better and more consistent results than virtually any other kind of diet for women in this age group. As of this writing, it has been used with resounding success with more than 7,000 women at Kaiser Permanente, and better than 75 per cent stick with it and succeed.

Findings from the original research, accepted and published in the *Journal of the American Dietetic Association*, received world-wide attention in the medical community, and practitioners from as far away as Israel and the Soviet Union have asked for details of the diet, citing similar complaints from female patients in the over-thirty-five category.

Some Success Stories

Approximately one-third of the women I've worked with in the programme are between the ages of thirty and forty. About half of my patients have been menopausal, post-menopausal or have had hysterectomies. Their backgrounds and experiences cover a wide range.

One patient was a secretary in her early thirties with a sedentary office job who had experienced a gradual weight gain over a period of years. She was wearing size-eighteen clothes when she started the 35-Plus Diet and went to size ten in eight months. As of this writing she's maintained her size-ten figure for three years.

Another young woman had experienced a typical rapid weight gain after her hysterectomy. Most of the added pounds collected around her middle, and her fashionable clothes no longer fitted. She'd put on fifteen pounds in four months, and took them off in three with the diet. The diet was 'a godsend', she said. 'Now I don't have to buy my clothes at the outsize shop anymore!' She's maintained her weight loss for five years.

Another patient, I'll call her Jane, gained twenty pounds when she quit smoking. She is a nurse and keenly aware of the health risks of smoking *and* the problems associated with being over-weight. What Jane particularly liked about the 35-Plus Diet were the 'chewables' offered by the unlimited vegetable list. She and her carrot sticks and broccoli buds got to be a joke around the office, but she lost the weight and now more than a year later is still a slender non-smoker.

One sixty-year-old patient came to me with high cholesterol levels and thirty pounds of excess weight. With the diet she lost the weight and brought her cholesterol count down to a safe level at the same time. Another patient in her later sixties had both high cholesterol *and* high blood-sugar. With the diet she lost twenty pounds and lowered both the cholesterol and blood-sugar levels. Three years later her weight, her cholesterol and blood-sugar are still under control.

One petite mother of three had always had some weight problems but nothing had ever done much to solve them. In her mid-thirties her weight gain began to accelerate, and by the age of thirty-eight she was thirty pounds overweight. With the diet she finally brought her weight under control, losing thirty pounds in eight months.

Two patients of mine in their early thirties are very active physically. Each had put on only about ten unwanted pounds, but in both cases the gain was all in the midriff and all their exercising wouldn't budge it. The 35-Plus Diet got rid of the bulge – and the ten pounds – on both women.

Another nurse among my patients – I'll call her Mary – is in her late thirties. Mary changed from a physically demanding job on the night shift to a desk job – a change in life style that put twenty pounds on her in six months. She shed them in five months with the diet, and as of writing this has kept them off for three years.

Pregnancy got the better of a patient I'll call Mrs Grayson, who gained far too much weight while she was carrying her baby. I put her on the diet after the baby was born, and she lost thirty pounds in six months. She looks terrific. I told her to be sure to come in for a special prenatal regime the next time she gets pregnant. I figure it won't be too long.

Some Features of the Diet:

Salt permitted While the diet doesn't promote profligate use of the salt shaker, neither does it rule salt out. Some current findings on the subject of sodium question the wisdom of urging universal salt restriction to the general population, and I concur with that thinking. Potassium, found in fruits and vegetables, is the other part of the sodium seesaw, and this diet promotes abundant use of potassium-containing produce. (An important exception here is the individual who is part of that subgroup of sodium-sensitive people for whom salt restriction is important and effective in lowering blood pressure. Follow your doctor's advice if you have a water-retention problem or hypertension related to salt intake.)

Meat permitted Including beef and other favourite red meats. This diet does not follow the popular fashion, arbitrarily excluding beef or pork or other meats, frequently without any justification. (Some cuts of meat actually have less fat and calories than some poultry parts, and it is these ultra-clean sources of protein that are favoured in the menus and recipes.)

Alcohol permitted Once you are into Phase Two. See Chapter 4 for details.

Controls hunger Attacking, allaying, forestalling and postponing hunger is a primary concern of any weight-loss diet, since the hungry dieter is soon an ex-dieter. This regimen works to prevent hunger on two fronts: at the table and away from it. At the table, by the liberal use of bulky, stomach-filling vegetables and other high fibre foods that prevent over-eating at meal times. To prevent nibbling between meals, the diet includes liberal amounts of slowly metabolized protein foods.

Deals with women's calcium needs Many diets that have been popular are actually all wrong for the 35-Plus Woman because they exacerbate the tendency for maturing women to develop the calcium deficiencies that ultimately lead to osteoporosis, the loss of bone mass that makes the bones of elderly women brittle and breakable. Current research informs us that this is a condition that has its roots in the eating habits of several decades earlier. Unfortunately, the drive toward slenderness usually deprives women of the very nutrients they need most, and many popular weight-loss diets further the damage.

Changes metabolism   The 35-Plus Diet deals with the chemistry of fluid retention and blood-sugar levels, and with another unseen and unrecognized enemy: the metabolic slow-down that results from excess fat. This is how weight gain not only becomes self-perpetuating but even picks up momentum as the weight problem remains unmanaged. This is how ten pounds turns into twenty and then fifty. The diet is designed to interrupt this vicious circle with a quick loss of water and fat. As the water flushes away and the fat melts, the metabolically inert burden disappears.

Nutritionally balanced   Unlike the high-protein fad diets of the 1960s and 1970s featured in bestselling diet books, this diet provides the basis for a lifetime of healthy eating.

Some of the differences:

The 35-Plus Diet   Is low in fat. No butter, margarine, oil or fat-adding ingredients are included, and the protein foods used are lean: chicken, poultry, fish, only lean fat-trimmed meat. (The fat high-protein diets of a decade ago called for large quantities of fatty steaks and hamburger.)

The 35-Plus Diet   Isn't overweight in protein. It allows about 80 grams per day; the typical nondieting woman may eat in excess of 100 grams. Some of the high-protein fads put no limit on protein intake.

The 35-Plus Diet   Does allow unlimited amounts of complex-carbohydrate vegetables – and fruit three times a day. Consequently, it's high in naturally occurring fibre. High-protein fad diets of the past generally made little mention of fibre or fibrous foods. In fact, they tended to discourage fibrous food intake by not differentiating between complex carbohydrate high-fibre vegetables and simple carbohydrate foods like sugar and refined flour.

The 35-Plus Diet Is enjoyable and easy to live with. It's versatile and flexible and fits into every life style. It's equally adaptable whether you love to cook or hate it.

THREE

The 35-Plus Diet

Here is the diet that has helped hundreds of women like you lose weight and keep it off. It's extremely simple to follow and very flexible. More than likely, you have everything on hand to begin this diet with your very next meal.

How the Diet is Organized

The diet is organized around three 'square' meals a day plus one anytime snack. If you generally eat your main meal at midday and a light supper in the evening, simply rearrange the diet schedule to make the second meal the main meal. The snack could be mid-morning coffee break, or late afternoon pick-me-up or a healthy after-dinner 'dessert'.

At each of these meals you are directed to eat a number of units or *servings* of different kinds of foods: lean protein, grain, fruit, etc. *Servings* generally apply to 1oz/25g or 1 unit (a peach, for example) or 4fl oz/100ml. More on that later.

As we have seen, the diet has three phases, each subsequent phase allowing more food than the preceding one. Although the differences are not great, they are critical! For example: Phase One dinner calls for a healthy portion of protein plus unlimited light vegetables, but no bread or other starches in the main meal. In Phase Two, dinner is augmented by one starch serving — bread, for example, or potatoes, pasta or rice.

Phase One is intended to jump-start your metabolism and turn it around into an energy-burning machine rather than one primed to store energy in the form of extra chins or flabby thighs. Phase One permits only two servings of starch food a day, one in the morning and one at lunch.

Phase One

You should stay on Phase One for one week. At the end of seven days, you will probably be pleased to see a dramatic weight loss on the scales. You may lose five pounds or more, depending on your body composition. Then you should proceed to Phase Two. The amount of weight loss varies with each individual. If you're a slow starter, you should not be discouraged because the amount of weight lost in the first week has little bearing on your ultimate success. My observation of hundreds of women on this diet discloses that some who lost the least weight at the beginning ultimately went on to achieve the most dramatic weight loss in the end.

If at the end of the first week you have lost less than two pounds, you should stay on Phase One for one more week —*but in no case should you stay on Phase One more than two weeks*.

Why is it important to limit Phase One to a maximum of two weeks? Because of the danger of ketosis.

The ratio of carbohydrate to protein and fat in Phase One is intended to bring the dieter to the *brink* of ketosis in order to force the body to relinquish its store of excess water between the cells. The body generally does this within a week (although some particularly stubborn cases of water retention may need a bit more time). Two weeks is the maximum duration for a diet that's severely restricted in necessary carbohydrates.

Phase Two

After the initial Phase One is over, the dieter moves on to Phase Two. At first glance, the difference seems small – one more slice of bread a day (or 2oz/50g of spaghetti) – but it is significant. The diet is carefully designed to provide just the right balance of lean protein and complex carbohydrate to foster the loss of fat and prevent a recurrence of waterlogging. For this reason, it's vital to follow the diet – exactly – in terms of portions and proportions of each type of food. Within those constraints, the diet is designed to provide maximum flexibility: you can interchange a wide variety of starch foods, enjoying corn on the cob one day and macaroni salad the next. But the diet will *not* work if you choose a second ear of corn instead of the grilled chicken, or if you decide to have less meat and more potatoes.

The ratio of protein to carbohydrate is important to keep the space between the cells squeezed dry of excess fluid. The amount of food you eat is important in retaining that ratio, as well as in keeping calories in check. Calories are important, but they have already been accounted for in the diet plan. If you eat more of a favourite food than the diet calls for – if you eat a food not permitted – you will sabotage your efforts both by over-consumption of calories and by destroying the protein-carbohydrate ratio that prevents water-weight gain.

– *How long should you stay on Phase Two?*   For as long as you need to, until you have reached your desirable weight (we'll discuss weight goals, later). Unlike unbalanced high-protein diets of the past, this is a safe, balanced diet that shortchanges only calories. So, as long as you have a ready supply of excess calories stored on your body, you can remain on Phase Two. This part of the diet is designed to draw on those fat reserves for energy, and to avoid replacing the lost fat by puffing up the spaces between the cells with water-weight gain.

Phase Three

After you have reached the weight you want to be, you are then faced with the most demanding and difficult challenge of all: maintaining that weight loss for the rest of your life. This is where nineteen out of twenty diets fail. The 35-Plus Diet meets that challenge successfully with a third phase that will last the rest of your life.

In Phase Three, we add 3 servings (3 teaspoons) of fats – other than saturated animal fats – to the diet. Stay on the diet five days a week. On the other two days – the weekend, for example – you can indulge yourself within reason by enjoying modest portions of foods not permitted on the diet. Remain on

Phase Three as long as your weight remains stable. If you regain more than five pounds, return to Phase Two and remain on it until the weight is lost.

After you have remained on Phase Three for more than two months without weight gain, you may add a third 'day off' to your programme, a mid-week day, for example, in which you might eat dinner out and enjoy a dessert. Or you might want to alternate days on and off your diet.

Again, if you regain more than five pounds, return to Phase Two and remain on it until the weight is lost, and then return to Phase Three with only two days off.

Phase Three is intended to help you find a happy, healthy level of food intake that can keep you well fed for the rest of your life without regaining those unwanted extra pounds. It's important to understand and accept that you will never be able to go back to your old eating habits – unless you are willing to go back to the weight you used to be!

PHASE ONE   (One to two weeks, maximum)
Number of Servings

Meal:	Breakfast	Lunch	Dinner	Anytime snack
Lean protein	1	3	6	—
Light vegetables	unlimited quantities, *at least 4 servings a day*			
Fruit	1	1	—	1
Skimmed milk/ yogurt	—	—	—	1
Grain/starch	1	1	none	none
Fats	none	none	none	none
Sugar	none	none	none	none
Alcohol	none	none	none	· none
Calcium supplement	1	1	2*	—
Vit/Min supplement	—	—	1*	—

PHASE TWO   (Until goal weight is achieved)
Number of Servings

Meal:	Breakfast	Lunch	Dinner	Anytime snack
Lean protein	1	3	6	—
Light vegetables	unlimited quantities, *at least 4 servings a day*			
Fruit	1	1	—	1
Skimmed milk/ yogurt	—	—	—	1
Grain/starch	1	1	1	—
Fats	none	none	none	none
Sugar	none	none	none	none
Alcohol	—	—	—	1 allowed
Calcium supplement	1	1	2*	—
Vit/Min supplement	—	—	1*	—

*Taken after dinner.

PHASE THREE (Five days a week, to stabilize and maintain permanent weight loss)
Number of Servings

Meal:	Breakfast	Lunch	Dinner	Anytime snack
Lean protein	1	3	6	–
Light vegetables	unlimited quantities, *at least 4 servings a day*			
Fruit	1	1	–	1
Skimmed milk/ yogurt	–	–	–	1
Grain/starch	1	1	1	–
Fats (mono & poly)	1	1	1	–
Sugar	none	none	none	none
Alcohol	–	–	–	1 allowed
Calcium supplement	1	1	2*	–
Vit/Min supplement	–	–	1*	–

*Taken after dinner.

Custom-Tailoring Your Menus

Three servings for lunch, six servings for dinner – does that mean three Quarter Pounders and six pork chops?

To make the diet easy to follow and maximize the flexibility among foods that are interchangeable, we've used an exchange system of units: small 'servings' that can range from 1oz/25g of meat to 4oz/100g of vegetables or fruit, to 4fl oz/100ml of milk. Although calories count – absolutely – this exchange system relieves you of the need to count them! You can make your choices from the Food List in the next chapter. This allows you the most freedom to design a diet to suit your own likes and dislikes, your own life style. Instead of a rigid one-size-fits-all diet – one that pinches and gaps and seems better suited to someone else – the 35-Plus Diet lets *you* custom-tailor menus and meal plans that meet your needs.

For example, the fruit and dairy foods under Anytime snack can be used anytime during the day – mid-morning coffee break, say, or late afternoon energizer. Or the foods and drinks listed could be added to regular meals. The fruit could be added to dinner, as dessert. The milk could be utilized in breakfast cereal or throughout the day in coffee. The one alcoholic beverage allowed in Phase Two could be light beer with lunch or dry wine with dinner or a pre-dinner cocktail or after-dinner brandy – pick one! It is also permissible to borrow 1oz/25g of protein from dinner – a thick slice of low-fat cheese, for example – and have that as part of a mid-morning or mid-afternoon snack.

A Diet for Men

Well, it needs some adaptation. This one is about 1,500 calories to accommodate differences in the male metabolism. If your man does physical labour or a lot of exercise, he may add additional servings of starch and fruit.

One feature of the Men's Diet is the addition of four servings of unsaturated fat. These include polyunsaturated margarine and vegetable oils such as corn and safflower oil, and monounsaturated fat such as olive oil. *I strongly urge that only unsaturated fats be used in the men's diet and that additional animal fat in the form of butter and cream be avoided.*

MEN'S DIET   (Approximately 1,500+ calories)
Number of Servings

Meal:	Breakfast	Lunch	Dinner	Anytime snack
Lean protein	1	3	6	1
Light vegetables	unlimited quantities, *at least 4 servings a day*			
Fruit	1	1	1	1
Skimmed milk/ yogurt	–	–	–	1
Grain/starch	2	2	2	1
Fats (unsaturated)	1	1	2	none
Sugar	none	none	none	none
Alcohol	none	none	none	1
Vit/Min supplement	–	–	–	1

FOUR

The 35-Plus-Diet Food Lists

LEAN PROTEIN FOOD LIST

MEAT

Lean Meat   One serving equals 1oz/25g (cooked).

Beef: fillet
        skirt
        mince, lean
        lean beef
        stewing steak
        lean-cut corned beef
        sirloin and rump steak
        silverside
        sirloin
        topside

Veal: most cuts

Lamb: chump chops, leg, loin chops, fat-trimmed minced,
        fillet

Pork: ham
        pork leg steaks
        pork fillet

Organ meats: liver (high cholesterol), limit to one 3-oz/75-g
        serving per month

Poultry: remove skin before or after cooking
        young frying chickens
        chickens
        guinea fowl
        pheasant
        young turkey

Luncheon meats:	most chicken and turkey alternatives
	light, lean luncheon meats 95 per cent to 98 per cent fat free
Game:	venison, most game except waterfowl

Medium-Fat Meat

Allowed no more than 3 times weekly. Trim carefully.

Beef:	chuck, rump, blade
Veal:	breast
Lamb:	cutlets, loin, best end of neck
Pork:	blade, hand and spring, neck end

Avoid:
High-Fat Cuts of Meat

Beef:	brisket
	corned beef brisket (lean-cut corned beef is permitted)
	forerib
	boneless forerib steak
	porterhouse, T-bone steak
	standard mince
Lamb:	breast of lamb
Pork:	minced pork
	sausage
	spareribs
Poultry:	capon, duck, goose, waterfowl
Luncheon meat:	standard frankfurters and hot dogs, pastrami, salami, veal loaf, most standard luncheon meats

FISH AND SHELLFISH

One serving equals 1oz/25g cooked, without bones, skin, or shells

Fish:	fresh and frozen: all varieties permitted
Shellfish:	raw, steamed, boiled, grilled or baked
	clams
	crabs
	crayfish
	mussels
	oysters
	scallops

canned:	tuna packed in water or brine
	salmon
	crabmeat
smoked:	cod, haddock, salmon, kippers, sturgeon, mackerel, etc.
pickled, cured:	salmon (lox)

Limit: no more than one 3-oz/75-g serving per week

sardines in tomato sauce
sardines
prawns
lobster

Avoid:
commercial breaded and fried fish
breaded and fried shellfish
herring in cream sauce
herring in sweet wine
sardines in oil
tuna packed in oil

DAIRY FOODS LIST

CHEESE

cottage cheese, low-fat (1 per cent or less)	*One serving equals:* 2½oz/60g
fresh farmhouse cheese, curd cheese	2½oz/60g
light or diet processed cheese	1oz/25g
Mozzarella, skimmed light and semi-skimmed	1oz/25g

Avoid: all full fat cheeses

Eggs

egg whites (1 serving equals 2 whites)
whole eggs (1 serving equals 1 large)

Limit: egg yolks and whole eggs (high in cholesterol) limit to 2 per week

Skimmed Milk and Yoghurt   *One serving equals:*

Milk:	skimmed, fresh	8fl oz/225ml
	skimmed, reconstituted	8fl oz/225ml
	skimmed, dried non-fat milk solids	
		4 tablespoons
	semi-skimmed milk, with less than 2 per cent fat	
		8fl oz/225ml
	milkshake mix, low-calorie sweetener	
		1 portion
	cocoa mix, low-calorie sweetener	
		1 portion
	buttermilk	8fl oz/225ml

Avoid: chocolate and other suger-sweetened milk drinks
double cream
single cream
semi-skimmed milk with 2 per cent fat or more
non-dairy creamers (dry, frozen, liquid)
whole milk

Yogurt:	plain skimmed milk yogurt	6oz/175g
	plain low-fat yogurt	6oz/175g

Avoid: whole milk yogurt
fruit yogurt sweetened with sugar or fructose

UNLIMITED VEGETABLES LIST

artichokes	chicory
asparagus	Chinese cabbage
aubergine	cos lettuce
bamboo shoots	courgettes
bean sprouts	cucumber
beetroots	curly endive
broccoli	dandelion leaves
Brussels sprouts	endive
cabbage	fennel
carrots	kohlrabi
cauliflower	leeks
celery	lettuce
chard	marrow

mixed vegetable juice (limit 8fl oz/
  225ml)
mushrooms
mustard leaves
okra
onions
peppers
pickles (dill, sour, or
  unsweetened)
radishes
sauerkraut
shallots

spinach
spring greens
summer squash: yellow, crook-
  neck, pattypan, spaghetti,
  scalloped
string beans (green or wax)
swedes
tomato juice (limit to 8fl oz/225ml)
tomatoes (limit to 1 medium)
turnip
watercress

GRAIN/STARCH LIST

Bread

One serving equals:

bagels	½ regular
bread sticks	2 (8-in/20-cm)
breadcrumbs	3 tablespoons
cracked wheat	1 slice
crispbread (high fibre)	2 pieces
English muffin	½ small
frankfurter bun	½ small
French	1 slice
hamburger bun	½ small
'light' calorie-reduced	2 slices
high fibre	2 slices
Italian	1 slice
pita pocket	1 ounce small
protein-enriched	1 slice
raisin bread	1 slice
roll, plain	1 half small
rye, pumpernickel	1 slice
tortilla, corn	1 (6-in/15-cm)
tortilla, wheat	½ (8-in/20-cm)
white	1 slice
whole wheat	1 slice

Avoid: biscuits
                    cake
                    coffee cake
                    cookies
                    corn muffins
                    cornbread
                    croissants
                    Danish pastry
                    doughnuts
                    fried croutons
                    French toast
                    pancakes
                    sweet rolls
                    waffles

Crackers

arrowroot	3
matzo	1 (6-in/15-cm diameter)
melba toast	4
pretzel sticks	25 (3-in/7.5-cm)
rye or wheat wafers	3(2- × 3½-in/8-cm)
water biscuits	4 (2½-in/6-cm squares)

Avoid: rich crackers
                    potato crisps
                    corn chips
                    fried snack chips

Starchy Vegetables, Cooked

beans, canned in sauce	2oz/50g
beans, dried, cooked	1½oz/40g dried weight
corn, kernels	⅓ cup
corn on the cob	1 small
broad beans, fresh	2oz/50g
broad beans, dried, cooked	1½oz/40g dried weight
lentils, dried, cooked	1½oz/40g dried weight

mixed vegetables	2oz/50g
parsnips	2oz/50g
peas, green	2oz/50g
peas, dried, cooked	1½oz/40g dried weight
potato baked with skin	1 small
potato, cooked and mashed	4½oz/125g
pumpkin, plain	6oz/175g
yam or sweet potato, plain	2oz/50g
winter squash	4oz/100g

Avoid: chips
sugary glazed yams, squash
sweet baked beans

Pasta

whole wheat	2oz/50g cooked
protein-enriched	2oz/50g cooked
egg noodles	2oz/50g cooked

Avoid: fried chow mein noodles

Cereal

oatmeal, cooked, plain	4oz/100g
most cooked cereals	4oz/100g
granola	1oz/25g
All-Bran	2oz/50g
bran flakes, 100 per cent	2oz/50g
Cheerios	3oz/75g
corn flakes, wheat flakes	3oz/75g
puffed wheat, corn or oats	2oz/50g
Special K	2oz/50g
most ready-to-eat cereals	3oz/75g

Avoid: sugar-coated cereals

Grains

barley, cooked	4oz/100g
bulgar, cracked wheat, cooked	4oz/100g
couscous, steamed	4oz/100g
popcorn, air-popped, no butter or oil	3oz/75g

rice, brown cooked	3½oz/85g
rice, white cooked	3½oz/85g
rice, wild cooked	3½oz/85g

Avoid: fried rice
packaged or prepared rice, pasta, potato, couscous
   or other grain convenience mixes with added fat

FRUITS LIST

*Fresh, frozen, or canned in water or unsweetened juice. May be sweetened with
   sugar substitute if desired.*

	One serving equals:
apple juice	2½fl oz/70ml
apples	1 small
apple sauce (sugar free)	8 tblsp
apricot halves	4oz/100g
apricot nectar	2½fl oz/70ml
apricots (dried)	4 halves
apricots (fresh)	2 medium
banana	½ small
blackberries	2oz/50g
blueberries	2oz/50g
boysenberries	2oz/50g
cherries	10
cider	2½fl oz/70ml
cranberry juice	2fl oz/50ml
dates	2
figs (dried)	1 small
figs (fresh)	1 large
fruit cocktail	4fl oz/100ml
fruit punch	2fl oz/50ml
gooseberries	2oz/50g
grape juice	2fl oz/50ml
grapefruit (fresh)	½ medium
grapefruit (juice)	4fl oz/100ml
grapefruit sections	5oz/150g
grapes	12 medium
Kiwi fruit	1 large or 2 small
loganberries	2oz/50g

mango	½ small
melon – watermelon	½ slice
melon – cantaloupe	¼ small
melon – honeydew	⅛ small
nectarine	1 small
orange	1 small
orange juice	4fl oz/100ml
orange segments	3½oz/85g
pawpaw	⅓ medium
peach (fresh or canned)	1 medium
pear (fresh or canned)	1 medium
persimmon	1 small
pineapple (canned)	1 large slice
pineapple (fresh)	3oz/75g
pineapple juice	2½fl oz/70ml
plums	2 medium
pomegranate (seeds)	¾ medium
prune juice	2fl oz/50ml
prunes	2 medium
raisins	2 tblsp
raspberries	2oz/50g
rhubarb (no sugar)	5oz/150g
strawberries	2oz/50g
tangerine	1 large or 2 small

FATS LIST

These foods and ingredients may be used only as directed in the recipes, and in Phase Three, and as directed in the Men's Diet.

Unsaturated Fats	*One serving equals:*
avocado	½ small
cooking oil (corn, olive, safflower, sunflower, etc.)	1 teaspoon
margarine (diet or whipped)	2 teaspoons
margarine (tub or block – first ingredients should be liquid oil)	1 teaspoon
mayonnaise	2 teaspoons
mayonnaise (light or calorie-reduced)	1 tblsp

nut butters, tahini	1 tblsp
nuts and peanuts, dry-roasted or oil-roasted	½oz/15g
peanut butter (all-natural)	1 tblsp
salad dressings (light low-fat, calorie reduced)	2 tblsp
salad dressings (bottled oil & vinegar type)	4 teaspoons
salad dressings (regular, bottled, mayonnaise-type)	1 tblsp
seeds (pumpkin or squash kernels, sunflower seed kernels)	½oz/15g
sour dressing, non-dairy	3 tblsp
wheat germ oil	1 tblsp

Saturated Fats

bacon (crisp)	1oz/25g
bacon fat	1 teaspoon
butter	1 teaspoon
chocolate, unsweetened baking	1oz/25g
coconut (shredded)	1oz/25g
coconut cream, unsweetened	3 tblsp
cream (single 10 per cent butterfat)	2 tblsp
cream (double 18 per cent butterfat)	1 tblsp
cream (sour)	2 tblsp
cream cheese (regular and whipped)	2 tblsp
cream cheese spreads	2 tblsp
cream substitute (liquid or dry)	2 tblsp
cream, whipped double (unsweetened)	2 tblsp
lard	1 teaspoon
margarines from hydrogenated fats (standard size block)	1 teaspoon
salt pork	½oz/15g

	sausagemeat or standard sausages	1oz/25g
	sauces and gravies, made with butter, fat or oil	5 tblsps

Avoid:

biscuits
cake
chow mein noodles
cookies
corn muffins
cornbread
cream crackers (high in fat)
croissants
doughnuts
frozen custard
frozen tofu desserts
frozen yogurt
fruit-flavoured yogurt with sugar
honey
ice-cream
ice milk
jam, jellies and preserves
lemonade, containing sugar
lemon ice, other sugar-sweetened fruit ices
molasses
muffins
pancakes
pies
potatoes, French fried
pudding and dessert mixes, sugar-sweetened jelly and gelatin desserts, sugar-sweetened sherbet
snack chips: potato, corn, etc.
soft-serve ice cream
sorbet
sugar: white, brown, fructose (fruit sugar), maple, demerara
sweet liqueurs and cordials (even if alcohol is permitted)
sweet pickles
sweet relish
sweet-and-sour sauces and glazes
sweetened, powdered drink mixes

sweet rolls (Danish pastry)
sweets
syrups
waffles
whipped cream, sugar-sweetened
whipped topping, non-dairy, sugar-sweetened
wine coolers (contain sugar)

Preparing Meals

Cooking Methods

Except as directed in the recipes, do not use any fat, oil, butter, margarine, shortening or high-fat ingredients in cooking. This means that frying and deep-fat frying, are out!

Meat, poultry, fish and seafood may be grilled, baked, roasted, steamed, stewed, microwaved, crock-potted, pressure-cooked, boiled or barbecued (no fat or sugary glazes added). Food may also be sautéed in a non-stick frying-pan, which has been coated with vegetable cooking oil.

You may cook vegetables, potatoes, or rice in stock, consommé or fat-free broth for flavour – no butter needed!

Permitted Seasonings

Salt is permitted, unless you are on a sodium-restricted diet. If you are, follow your doctor's advice. He or she may suggest that you omit salt and use a salt substitute and such alternative ingredients as salt-free stock.

Experiment with seasonings to make your food interesting. You may also use any of the following:

lemon juice	lime juice
mustard	horseradish
herbs	spices
sugar substitutes	baking powder
baking soda	unsweetened cocoa powder

coffee
decaffeinated coffee
plain gelatin
sugar-free gelatin mixes

beverages (sugar-free)
vinegar
sugar-free powdered drink
mixes

Provided you are under no additional diet restrictions, you may use the following condiments in the specified amounts:

cereal beverage, like Ovaltine	1 tablespoon
ketchup, barbecue sauce or chilli sauce	1 tablespoon
relish	1 tablespoon
soy sauce	2 tablespoons
steak sauce	2 tablespoons

Permitted Beverages

You may drink all of the following you want:

regular or decaffeinated coffee, black*
tea, herbal tea, iced tea (sugar-free)*
water (soda water or mineral water may be substituted)
diet lemonade*

Note: You may wish to use the milk allowed with the diet in the beverages above.

Sugar-Free Milk Drinks   Be aware that some of the sugar-free products, like the hot cocoa drinks, do contain milk. If you drink them, subtract them from your daily milk allowance.

Alcoholic Beverages   Please do not drink any alcoholic beverages for the first two weeks. Thereafter, you should limit yourself to just one drink a day.
   Use the following amounts:

1fl oz/25ml spirits
          or
4fl oz/100ml dry wine
          or
1 light beer

*See Chapter 2 for information on the effects of caffeine.

Alcoholic beverages simply add calories to your diet, nothing more. And this diet changes your body chemistry, so one drink will have the effect of two.

Caution: Wine coolers and cream liqueurs contain sugar, and some drinks contain added fat. Coolers and punches sweetened with sugar are off limits. So are sweet and creamy after-dinner drinks that contain cream as well as sugar. Beware sugar-mixed drinks like whisky sours and margaritas, and piña coladas that contain both sugar and fat in the form of sweetened coconut cream.

Alcohol-free wines and beers are also permitted (limited to one a day).

FIVE

Putting It All Together: Sample Menus

Whether you love to cook or hate it, never eat out or never eat at home, adore spicy food or can't abide it, this diet can be adapted to fit your likes and life style. Here are some menu suggestions to start you thinking.

Menu I

Breakfast

¼ small cantaloupe melon
2½oz/65g low-fat cottage cheese
4 pieces of melba toast (rye or whole wheat)
Beverage of your choice

Lunch

3 oz/75g turkey breast
1 small pita bread (whole wheat)
1 tablespoon high-protein, low-fat mayonnaise
Lettuce
Carrot or celery sticks or cucumber slices
1 large peach
Beverage of your choice

Dinner

6oz/175g barbecued beef skirt or rump steak,
cooked in one of the marinade sauces
Grilled tomato
Green beans and carrots in broth
(Phase Two: 3½oz/85g brown or white rice cooked in stock)
Fresh spinach salad with mushrooms and bean sprouts
Slim Vinaigrette Dressing (see page 133)
Beverage of your choice

Snack

3oz/75g strawberries or other soft fruit
6oz/175g plain yogurt, with sweetener, if desired

Menu II

Breakfast

½ small banana
2oz/50g raisin bran or All-Bran
4fl oz/100ml skimmed milk
1oz/25g slice ham, grilled
Beverage of your choice

Lunch

Seafood Fried Rice (see page 121)
Lettuce and tomato salad, light dressing of your choice
A crisp, red apple
Beverage of your choice

Dinner

Aubergine Parmesan (see page 136)
(Phase Two: 1 thin slice Italian bread)
Very large tossed salad
Slim Vinaigrette Dressing (see page 133)
Beverage of your choice
(Phase Two: 4fl oz/100ml of dry wine, optional)

Snack

Melon in season
1oz/25g Yogurt Cheese (see page 184)

Menu III

Breakfast

4fl oz/100ml orange juice
1 poached egg
1 slice of dry toast (raisin or whole wheat)
Beverage of your choice

Lunch

Sandwich: 2oz/50g lean ham
1oz/25g semi-skimmed Mozzarella cheese
2 slices of very thin bread or diet bread (toasted)
Lettuce, 2 tablespoons Light and Creamy Russian
Dressing (see page 132) on sandwich
Garnish with raw vegetables and pickles
3oz/75g fresh or canned sugar-free pineapple
Beverage of your choice

Dinner

8fl oz/225ml home-made or canned chicken broth with chopped
carrots and celery
Spicy Sweet and Sour Meatballs (see page 143)
served with steamed cabbage, shredded
Pickled beetroots in vinaigrette dressing
(Phase Two: 1 small crisp roll)
Beverage of your choice

Snack

6oz/175g plain yogurt
2 tablespoons granola

Menu IV

Breakfast

8fl oz/225ml V8 juice
1 scrambled egg made with 2 tablespoons skimmed milk,
¼ teaspoon dry mustard, cooked in a non-stick pan coated with
cooking oil
1 slice rye toast (dry)
Beverage of your choice

Lunch

3oz/75g roast beef on small pita bread with
mustard and lettuce
Green pepper ring, radishes and spring onion
1 orange
8fl oz/225ml low-fat milk or buttermilk

Dinner

Baked cod (5oz/150g) brushed with lemon juice
and light mayonnaise
Steamed courgette
(Phase Two: 2oz/50g green peas)
Cucumber in vinaigrette dressing
No-Cook Chocolate Mousse (see page 188)
Beverage of your choice

Snack

2oz/50g fresh or thawed raspberries
2oz/50g low-fat cottage cheese
Optional: sug? substitute to taste

Menu V

Breakfast

½ grapefruit
1oz/25g granola
6oz/175g plain yogurt
1oz/25g boiled ham, lean
Beverage of your choice

Lunch

8oz/225g low-fat cottage cheese served on lettuce with
chopped-up vegetables (cucumber, radishes, spring onions,
carrots and celery)
½ toasted bagel (dry)
1 sweet, ripe pear
Beverage of your choice

Dinner

Chicken and Peppers (see page 146)
Summer squash or courgette
2 bread sticks
Large, tossed salad with herbs and low-fat dressing
Beverage of your choice

Snack

1 crisp apple
1oz/25g farmhouse or Yogurt Cheese (see page 184)

Menu VI

Breakfast

4fl oz/100ml grapefruit juice
½ toasted whole wheat English muffin (dry)
1 soft-boiled egg
Sugar-free hot chocolate

Lunch

3oz/75g very lean corned beef, on 1 slice rye bread
Prepared mustard
Large dill pickle
½ bottle no-alcohol beer (or beverage of your choice)
2 fresh plums

Dinner

Oven Shish Kebab (see page 144) with 6oz/175g lean lamb
(Phase Two: 2oz/50g cooked noodles)
Salad of 5oz/150g grated carrots, diet dressing on a bed of
lettuce
Summer Squash, Turkish Style (see page 169)
Luscious Lime Parfait (see page 195)

Snack

1 wholewheat cracker
1oz/25g smoked Mozzarella
(or any processed low-fat cheese made from skimmed milk)

Menu VII: Sunday

Brunch

⅛ of Quiche Lorraine (see page 120)
Fruit salad of ½ orange, ¼ banana, 3oz/75g pineapple,
2oz/50g plain yogurt as dressing – low-calorie sweetener
optional
Grilled tomato half sprinkled with Parmesan cheese
and sweet basil
½ bagel, spread with a teaspoon of cottage cheese
blended with chives
Cinnamon coffee or herbal tea

Afternoon Cocktail Hour

4 melba toast
1oz/25g Yogurt Cheese (see page 184)
Celery stuffed with 2½oz/60g cottage cheese with chives
(Phase Two: 4fl oz/100ml dry white wine,
or 1fl oz/25ml vodka, gin, scotch or other spirits
with water, soda water or diet lemonade)

Dinner

5oz/150g lean ham steak, grilled or sautéed in a non-stick
frying pan
(Phase Two: ½ baked sweet potato)
Mixed vegetables cooked in stock (carrots, Brussels
sprouts and cauliflower, for example)
Salad of onion, tomato and vinaigrette dressing
on a bed of lettuce
Beverage of your choice

Snack (Dessert)

1 slice of Fruited Cheesecake (see page 191)

'I Hate to Cook' Menus
Menu I

Breakfast
(can be packed for work)

1 orange
6 crackers or four slices of melba toast (whole wheat or rye)
1oz/25g low-fat cheese
Coffee, tea or beverage of your choice

Lunch
(can be bought or brought from home)

Sandwich: 3oz/75g turkey
2 slices reduced-calorie bread
2 teaspoons low-calorie mayonnaise (pickles, lettuce,
tomatoes permitted)
1 apple, unpeeled, cut in wedges
Beverage of your choice

Dinner

One quarter of a roasted chicken, skin removed
(buy ready-cooked on the way home from work)
Very large tossed salad (diet dressing only)
(Phase Two: 2 bread sticks, whole wheat or rye)
⅛ of a honeydew melon (or other unsweetened fruit of
your choice)
Beverage of your choice

Snack

6oz/175g plain low-fat yogurt (add a few drops of vanilla,
some crushed fruit and sweeten to taste with sugar
substitute if you like)
or
1 portion sugar-free milk shake, prepared
according to packet directions

Menu II

Breakfast
(may be packed or eaten at home)

4fl oz/100ml orange juice
1 hard- or soft-boiled egg
1 slice raisin or whole-wheat bread (plain or toasted)
Beverage of your choice

Lunch
(can be bought or made at home)

8fl oz/225ml vegetable soup
1 plain hamburger with lettuce, tomato, pickle, etc.
on ½ bun or tucked in a 1oz/25g pita pocket
1 pear
Beverage of your choice

Dinner

Grilled, small (8oz/225g) boneless sirloin steak —
equals 6oz/175g cooked
(Phase Two: small baked potato, topped with yogurt
and chopped parsley, or chives)
6oz/175g green beans, cooked (fresh, frozen or canned)
Salad (may be made fresh or left over from
another meal)
Beverage of your choice
(Phase Two: 4fl oz/100ml dry red wine, optional)

Snack

Skimmed milk
Apple
1oz/25g cheese

Menu III

Breakfast

½ banana or 2oz/50g berries
2oz/50g All-Bran, Corn Flakes or Special K
4fl oz/100ml skimmed milk
Beverage of your choice

Lunch
(bought or made at home)

3oz/75g sliced lean ham and low-fat Swiss cheese
on 1 slice of rye bread, with mustard
Mixed salad – 2 tablespoons diet dressing
2oz/50g unsweetened fresh or canned fruit (no syrup)
Beverage of your choice

Dinner

Large salad niçoise, including fresh vegetables,
salad greens, raw green beans plus 3oz/75g can
water-packed tuna
2 hard-boiled eggs
2 tablespoons low-calorie salad dressing
(Phase Two: 4 pieces rye melba toast or crispbread
broken into croutons)
Beverage of your choice
(Phase Two: 8fl oz/225ml light beer, optional)

Snack

1 crisp apple
1oz/25g low-fat Cheddar cheese
1 portion sugar-free hot cocoa

Menu IV

Breakfast

½ grapefruit
1oz/25g ham
1 slice bread (or ½ whole wheat bagel)
Beverage of your choice

Lunch

3oz/75g corned beef (lean cut only) on 1 slice
rye bread or 2 slices diet bread
Pickle (sour or dill)
Small salad
(You can save your fruit for an afternoon break)
Beverage of your choice

Dinner

(Phase Two: 8fl oz/225ml chicken noodle soup)
6oz/175g lean roast beef (bought at delicatessen)
1×10oz/275g packet frozen broccoli, cooked and seasoned with
lemon and pepper
Sliced tomato and cucumber salad
Beverage of your choice

Snack

6oz/175g plain yogurt
1oz/25g fresh or frozen blueberries
2 tablespoons granola
Optional: sugar substitute to taste

SIX

Carbohydrates, Proteins, Fats and Fibre: A Crash Course in Nutrition

You are what you eat – it's not just a saying. Food literally becomes you. Food is our primary tool for building strong bodies. Some knowledge of the basic facts of nutrition is helpful to everyone.

Except for the water we drink and the oxygen we breathe, the needs of the body can only be met by food. To nourish the body, food has three vital jobs:

- To provide fuel (calories) the body can burn to set free the energy needed for activity.
- To provide the building materials needed to make or maintain body tissue.
- To provide substances that help regulate body processes.

All foods are compounds, mixtures of chemicals found in nature, and these nourishing natural chemicals are known as nutrients. There are six classes of nutrients the body needs:

- Carbohydrates
- Proteins
- Fats
- Vitamins
- Minerals
- Water

All six are equally important.

Regardless of where you live on this earth – Kalamazoo, Katmandu or Kuala Lumpur – no matter what the cuisine, you need all six nutrients.

The first three — carbohydrates, proteins and fats — are the fuel nutrients, sources of calories. They are the only substances that the body can burn to supply energy for work and heat.

Carbohydrates

Carbohydrates are either simple sugars or more complex compounds, such as starch. All food carbohydrates except lactose (milk sugar) are formed in the vegetable kingdom.

The sweet taste of corn and peas is due to its natural sugar — sugar that will turn to starch when overripe. Sometimes it works the other way round: some fruits, bananas for example, contain starch that turns to sugar on ripening. Carrots, beetroots, onions, winter squash, turnips and sweet potatoes are all vegetables that contain appreciable amounts of natural sugar. Fruits are rich in natural sugar; that's why they're naturally sweet.

However, few foods in nature are as intensely sweet as refined white table sugar, or the candies, sweets and snacks we have come to indulge in. In nature, sugar exists as part of a balanced 'package'. A sun-ripened peach plucked from the tree contains not only sugar but fibre, flavour, juice and vitamins, particularly vitamin A. The natural sugar in fruits and vegetables comes packaged with so much water and bulky fibre that it's difficult to overindulge in sugar from totally natural sources.

In refining sugar for table use, what we have done, essentially, is to separate the pure, refined carbohydrate — the calories — from everything else of value in terms of nourishment and appetite control. The moisture, vitamin and bulk are discarded. What remains is a refined, white granulated substance with no nutritional value except calories. Refined sugar is simple carbohydrate, rapidly absorbed by the body.

What we tend to do with this refined, white substance is to sprinkle and stir it into foods, making them sweeter than nature ever intended, thereby overburdening our bodies with an unnatural sugar load. This can have dire consequences for some people, contributing to the excessive rise in blood fats and blood-sugar levels associated with heart disease and diabetes.

Sucrose and Fructose

Our sugar supply for table use and cooking comes chiefly from juices of the sugar cane or sugar beet. Sugar obtained from cane, sugar beets and sap from the sugar maple tree are all sucrose – ordinary white table sugar. We often hear about another, supposedly healthier, form of sugar: fructose, also known as fruit sugar. Granulated fructose and fructose syrups are sold in health food stores. High fructose corn syrup (refined from corn, as its name suggests) is being used in the food industry as a less expensive alternative to sucrose. The molecular differences between sucrose and fructose permit the latter to perform somewhat differently and give it a minor edge over sucrose as a sweetener for the weight conscious. Although both have identical calorie counts (16 per level tea-spoon), fructose has more sweetening power than sugar when used with fruit or other acid-containing ingredients. Therefore you may need only half as much – half the calories' worth – of fructose to sweeten strawberry yogurt. However there would be no calorie savings in using fructose in vanilla mousse or chocolate cake because neither are acidic. Fructose is also absorbed more slowly than sucrose, making it less likely to raise blood-sugar levels.

However fructose, like sucrose, is a refined carbohydrate, and like sucrose, it's pure calories. In this diet, where carbo-hydrates are kept in careful balance with protein in order to remedy water retention, there are no calories to waste on either fructose or sucrose. Only the natural fruit sugar that comes as part of a balanced package – an apple or orange, for example – is permitted. (Sugar substitutes are virtually free of calories and carbohydrates and may be used to augment sweetness for those with an unreformable sweet tooth!)

Honey, molasses, brown sugar, demerara sugar
These are simply other forms of sugar, and are used by the body as sugar. They are also off limits on the 35-Plus Diet.

Starches

Starch is more complex than sugar. Starches are formed in plants by the union of many molecules of glucose, a form of sugar. Starch is the carbohydrate found in seeds, tubers and roots where plants store it for future energy needs. In the plant, starch is laid down in granules coated with a cellulose-like substance, and different plants have granules of characteristic size and shape.

When you cook starch granules, the cells absorb water, swell and rupture. They are more easily digested in this state. Therefore, before starch can be used as a source of energy, it must be broken down into simple sugar. Cooking helps start the process so our bodies can finish the work. Our chief sources of starch are grains and the products made from them (breads, cereals, pasta, etc.) legumes (beans and peas) and certain tuber and root vegetables (potatoes and sweet potatoes).

Protein

Proteins are present in all living tissues – plant or animal – and they are essential to life. Proteins are a vital part of the nucleus and protoplasm of every cell. The human body is made up of a variety of specialized proteins, keratin, for example. The outer layers of skin, the hair and the nails consist almost entirely of keratin.

The most native and abundant tissues of the body – the muscles and glandular organs – are high in protein content. Blood, of course, carries the important protein haemoglobin in its red cells and several proteins in solution in fluid (plasma) portions.

Protein molecules are a kind of 'mosaic' made up of nitrogen-containing compounds called amino acids.

Certain amino acids are said to be essential – that is, they must be already formed and present in the food. In reality, all amino acids are essential to the human body. However, the body can make at least some of them itself if necessary. For that reason, an amino acid is referred to as 'essential' (indispensable) only if your body can't make it for itself.

It should be made clear that a vegetarian diet can provide adequate protein if a wide enough variety of vegetable proteins is eaten. In combination these can supplement each other to furnish adequate amounts of all essential amino acids.

It is extremely important to remember that protein, a valuable substance for both plants and animals, is not stored in large amounts. The supply should be *replenished daily*.

Fat

The high calorie count of fat (weight for weight more than twice that of carbohydrate or protein) means that relatively small amounts of fatty foods can quickly raise the caloric bottom line of the day's food intake. For that reason, fats are useful in a weight-*gaining* diet, or when it's desirable to have a high-calorie intake with little bulk. Whenever you eat more calories than you burn off – whether the food is fat, protein or carbohydrate – the extra calories are converted into body fat and stored in various parts of the body.

Fat deposits in the human body are good or bad according to whether they are moderate or excessive. Some fat under the skin and about the organs serves a useful purpose, historically as a reserve store of fuel in time of need. Moderate fat also helps support organs, protects them from injury and prevents loss of body heat. But an overfed person goes on storing fat that will never be needed.

Fibre

Fibre is not a true nutrient because much of it is indigestible and therefore it doesn't 'nourish'. But vegetable fibre or cellulose is very important for a variety of reasons. Adding fibre foods to the diet is one of the best ways to cut calories without hunger.

Fibre fills you up – not out. But fibre is more than bran flakes.

Fibre is an entire family of substances from a wide variety of vegetable sources. Different kinds of fibre produce different results and offer different benefits. To eat well and lose weight safely, as well as enjoyably, you'll want to add a variety of fibre foods to the menu every day.

Fibre comes from vegetables, fruits and whole grains. In fact, fibre is found *only* in 'growing foods' – food from the earth – never in such animal foods as meat, fish, poultry, eggs, cheese or milk. Cheap meat may be tough, stringy and fibrous, but no animal food contains any dietary fibre whatsoever. That's because dietary fibre comes from the cell walls of plants. It includes such substances as cellulose, lignin, pectins and gums.

Bran

Bran, the best known source of fibre, contains cellulose and lignin. But even bran offers a choice of sources. More than likely, the bran in your breakfast cereal or bran muffin comes from wheat, milled from the coarse outer layer of the wheat kernel. This is the dark, coarse part that's ground off in the manufacture of white-bread flour. But bran can also be made from other grains: the outer layer of corn kernels, oats, soya beans, peas or rice. Corn bran has a mild flavour and light colour; rice bran is high in protein.

Whatever their source, all kinds of bran share a traditional claim to fame: the promotion of regularity. Constipation is the unpleasant and all-too-common outcome of a junk-food diet. Calorie-dense, refined foods tend to compress and compact in the bowels. The addition of bran to the diet helps alleviate this uncomfortable condition by adding bulk or 'roughage'. Bulk helps to increase the speed of elimination.

You are also getting the benefit of bran when you eat whole grains, because the unprocessed grains have the valuable bran layer left intact.

Pectin

Other kinds of fibre come from fruits and vegetables. These are the water-retaining gums and pectins that are a normal part of the outer structure of plant cells. Pectin is best known for its ability to cause fruit purées to jell. Cooks make use of this characteristic in the making of jam. Just as pectin performs its action by holding water in suspension, gums and pectins do the same thing in the intestine, helping to forestall constipation and the production of hard, dry, compacted stools. Pectin is a natural softener. It's particularly abundant in the peels of apples and the skins of citrus fruits.

Health Benefits of a High-Fibre Diet

In recent years these beneficial regularity-promoting features of fibre have been shown to have other equally important health benefits. Because fibre helps to speed waste through human plumbing, internal body tissues spend less time in contact with potentially hazardous cancer-causing agents that may be in the food supply. And the gums and pectins found in fruits and vegetables help to prevent the absorption of cholesterol from animal foods, reducing blood-cholesterol levels.

There are particular benefits for diabetics and hypoglycaemia sufferers. Roughage helps to dilute and slow down the absorption of sugar into the bloodstream, thereby making it possible for some to reduce their insulin dependency. This same blood sugar regulating effect is important to dieters because blood sugar and insulin levels have an impact on hunger and sugar-cravings.

High-fibre dining is also said to help to lower cholesterol, lessen the risk of bowel cancer, and protect against colitis, appendicitis, haemorrhoids and varicose veins.

A low-fat, high-fibre diet is recommended by the American Cancer Society, the American Heart Association and the American Diabetes Association.

For 35-Plus Dieters, tricked by their metabolism into hungering for more food than they can utilize, the appetite-appeasement feature of fibre foods makes them real winners. High-fibre foods are generally low-fat and calorie-light, puffed-up by nature with a healthy proportion of indigestible bulk. This bonus bulk satisfies the need to chew and fills the stomach, but it leaves the body without being metabolized or stored as unwanted body fat.

Enjoying fibre-rich dishes can help cut calorie intake and absorption. The fibre in food attracts and holds water, creating a sensation of fullness. Better yet, fibre speeds food through your system, helping to eliminate some of the nutrients before they can be completely absorbed.

The 35-Plus Diet is a low-fat, high-fibre diet. When talking to my patients, I describe myself as a vegetable-pusher. I insist they eat more cooked as well as raw vegetables. Vegetables raise fibre intake and help fight the 'hungries'.

SEVEN

Calcium: A Woman's Special Problem

It's been drummed into us since childhood that milk and other calcium-containing foods are important to build strong bones and teeth during the growth period of youth. Now there's new understanding that an adequate intake of calcium is just as important in the adult years, to aid in the prevention of osteoporosis. This potentially crippling breakdown of bone tissue in midlife and beyond is truly a woman's disease. The fact that it does chiefly attack women — middle-aged and older women at that — may explain why osteoporosis did not, until, recently, garner as much attention as male-threatening heart disease.

It's quite common for women approaching midlife to begin suffering from a slow but relentless washing away of bone. This is the primary cause of such bone deformities as the dowager's hump in elderly women and also makes the bones more likely to break with injury. While the causes of this bone loss are still not completely understood, several important factors have been identified:

● Lack of exercise. Without sufficient exercise to put stress on the bones, they will soften regardless of what else is done. The exercise must be weight-bearing. That's why walking has out-ranked swimming as the ideal, all-purpose exercise.
● Lack of calcium in the diet. For various reasons, mature women often do not take in enough calcium to allow the body to keep the bones strong.

● Lack of female hormone (oestrogen). After menopause, women become much more prone to osteoporosis. There is evidence that oestrogen replacement can help reverse this. However, taking oestrogen may increase the risk of cancer of the uterus. Consequently, putting a postmenopausal woman on oestrogens is not an automatic treatment but is done only after the woman and her doctor carefully evaluate the risks and benefits of the individual case.

● Other factors such as race and heredity. The risk of osteoporosis is highest in white women and lowest in black men.

Exercising Care for Your Bones

We can't change our race and sex. And we'll want to think long and hard about taking hormones. But we can begin right now taking steps − literally and figuratively − to preserve our bones. Even if you are a total couch potato, you can begin today by taking a walk to the end of the block. Tomorrow add another block. And continue adding blocks until you are taking a one-hour walk every day. After that you can begin working on your speed, gradually increasing the number of blocks you can walk in one hour. This simple fitness programme is easy to maintain anywhere, no matter where you live, work or travel. If need be, you can even walk around the same block several times, in circles, or up and down the same block. Walking indoors for an hour has the same effect; if necessary, in bad weather you might walk the corridors of your office building. I know a frequent flyer who walks airport terminals between flights.

Fighting osteoporosis should be reason enough to begin an exercise programme. When you add it to all the other, perhaps better-known motivations, it's apparent that exercise is of paramount importance to the 35-Plus Woman. Consider these other benefits:

● You'll help protect your heart. As women approach midlife, they need to remember that the heart-saving hormonal advantage they have had over men will eventually decline. Past

menopause, women's risk of heart disease is similar to that of men.
- You'll feel better. Exercise is a great mood elevator. It's easier to remain on a diet when your outlook is optimistic.
- You'll be less hungry. Inactivity impairs the body's natural appetite control mechanism.
- You'll lose weight faster if you exercise.
- You'll look thinner at the same weight than if you didn't exercise.
- You'll speed up your metabolism, lessening the likelihood that you'll regain the weight lost.

Adding Calcium to Your Diet

To maintain good bone strength, you need 1,000 to 1,500mg of calcium a day in your diet. The best source of calcium is dairy products.

Dairy Products	Calcium
8fl oz/225ml skimmed milk	359mg
8fl oz/225ml whole milk	298mg
1oz/25g hard cheese	218mg
1oz/25g low-fat soft cheese	158mg
4oz/100g cottage cheese (low fat)	105mg
8oz/225g yogurt (skimmed milk, plain)	293mg

Non-dairy Products	Calcium
2oz/50g green leafy vegetables (broccoli, kale, spring greens, spinach, mustard leaves, dandelion leaves)	50–180mg
8oz/225g whole wheat flour	49mg
8oz/225g white enriched flour	20mg
4oz/100g dried beans	75–150mg

Ideally, a well-planned diet should provide enough calcium to meet minimum daily requirements; however, experience has shown that with older people, many of whom have trouble digesting milk and some milk products, it may be difficult to take in adequate calcium through meals alone. If you are unable to get 1,000 to 1,500mg calcium a day in your diet, you should seriously consider using a calcium supplement.

Of the many calcium supplements available, calcium carbonate is inexpensive and effective. An excellent and inexpensive source of calcium carbonate is Tums. Four regular strength or three extra strength Tums should provide all the extra calcium you need, but if it fails to work for you – some women experience an uncomfortable gassy feeling – experiment with other preparations. If you are going to use a calcium supplement please note the following:

● Avoid high-priced products, particularly those sold in health food stores. They are no more safe or effective than plain calcium carbonate.
● Anyone with a history of kidney stones should check first with her doctor before taking extra calcium.

On the other hand, if you cannot tolerate supplements, then you should manipulate the protein allowance in the diet to increase your calcium intake. Use three servings (3oz/75g) of your daily protein allowance in the form of low-fat cheese. When the cheese is added to the 8fl oz/225ml of milk called for by the 35-Plus Diet, that will give you 4 servings of milk foods a day.

Vitamin D

Vitamin D is required by the body, in addition to calcium, for the formation of strong bones. Vitamin D is found in the diet in dairy products. It is also found in large amounts in fish oils. Your body can manufacture its own Vitamin D if you are exposed to enough sunlight.

If you cannot tolerate dairy products and are not exposed to much sunlight, you may obtain extra Vitamin D by taking *one* multiple vitamin tablet a day. This should be taken with a meal. If taken in excess amounts, Vitamin D can be *toxic* so do not exceed recommended dosage.

Substances That Interfere With Body Calcium Levels

Certain substances tend to reduce body calcium levels by acting in a variety of ways. Those substances include:

- antacids that contain aluminium
- cortisone-type drugs in large doses
- caffeine in large amounts (coffee, tea, cola beverages, some pain relievers)
- nicotine (tobacco)
- alcoholic drinks
- fad diets very high in protein

None of these substances will cause harm with occasional use. However, heavy users should discuss their calcium needs with their doctors.

EIGHT

The Pleasure Principle

There's an aspect of the 35-Plus Woman's life that I suspect may have subtle but profound effects on her physical well-being as well as her emotions. I call it the pleasure principle. There are no scientific studies to support my guess, but my observations tend to suggest that the less of it a woman has in her life – pleasure, that is – the more likely she is to run into problems, including weight problems. Yes, I am talking about sexual fulfilment, but that's just one of a whole range of pleasures that I sense are sadly missing from some women's lives.

But let's talk about that one first.

I don't conduct research into the sex lives of my patients. In fact I never bring up the topic. But in the course of seeing hundreds of women in my office and in classes, I sometimes do get to know quite a bit about their private lives. What's clear to me is that many women, including many young women in their thirties, have simply ceased to function sexually.

Some women confide in distress that their husbands are no longer interested in them. Even more worrisome, perhaps, are the women who are themselves no longer interested.

Here's a tip-off to the sexually dead relationship. When I ask a woman how her husband feels about her weight, she replies, 'He's used to me.' As if she were wallpaper.

Sexual Disconnection

Why is it, do you suppose, that these women seem so turned off, so out of touch with their sexuality? And which came first? The weight problem followed by sexual disconnection? Or did they cease being sexual beings and then gain weight? This isn't a test; I honestly don't know the answer myself. But I find it worth considering.

It's possible to imagine a couple of different scenarios of how this sexual extinction might come to be.

In one scene, she puts on weight, and that turns him off. To avoid sexual confrontation, he falls asleep on the sofa or stays out late. Or hangs out at the office or the neighbourhood pub. He may drink excessively or otherwise behave boorishly to make himself so unattractive that the sexual abstinence seems like her idea. Or he may simply rebuff her advances, something so humiliating to a woman that she stops asking – and ultimately stops wanting. To save her ego she becomes sexually numb.

Or in another variation of the same play, she puts on weight and turns herself off. She feels flabby and sexually unattractive. In the bedroom even with the lights off, she's so focused on her imagined physical shortcomings that she's completely unable to respond to her mate's advances. Sex becomes an ordeal for both of them, and they stop trying.

And then there's another intriguing and even more complex scenario: the one in which she – or he or they – lose interest in sex first. And then she gains weight. This is particularly fascinating for the number of questions it raises. Why do some people turn off sexuality in the prime of life? Is it particular to the relationship – they're not getting along for whatever reasons – or is it a widespread symptom of the fast-trackers' over-extended appointment book? And why do some women respond to the stress in their lives and the absence of sexual fulfillment by gaining weight? Is it simply a matter of substituting chocolate bars for sexual pleasure? Or is it more complicated? Does the premature shutdown in sexuality induce – prematurely – at least some of the hormonal changes that contribute to weight gain?

I can't pretend to know the answers or even all the questions about how the pleasure principle relates to 35-Plus weight problems, but I do know that things tend to change dramatically in this regard as the excess weight is lost. It's truly a delight for me to observe one of these sexually asleep women beginning to stir and emerge from her hibernation. She starts wearing make-up again and styling her hair. The first outward manifestations may be something as simple as nail polish, or wearing a dress to class instead of the same old baggy jeans. Quite simply she starts looking prettier and smiles more. She may let it be known, through jokes and innuendo, that she's sexually alive again.

If I had to give advice on this aspect, I'd go with the likely. I'd suggest that keeping one's sexuality alive – by whatever means – is probably beneficial in ways that we may not yet understand. The mind and body work in concert and the counsel to 'use it or lose it' probably relates to sex as well as exercise.

The first step in fulfilling this prescription is often simply to make the time. I am honestly aghast at the burdens some 35-Plus Women are carrying and their grim determination to be superwoman.

Permissible Pleasures

Sexual fulfilment is only one of a whole range of pleasures that may be missing from some women's lives. With the responsibilities some of these women carry – attending to demanding mates, raising children, caring for parents, maintaining houses, competing in corporations or professions, building for the future – there seems to be no 'self' time left over. No time to indulge the senses except in the kitchen or when they sit down to a meal. Music? For many, the only time to listen to music is in the elevator on the way to the office. Movies? Flowers? Art? Leisure time is curtailed for the executive, and the creative expressions that homemakers used to enjoy as part of their job description are left undone or assigned to professionals.

Food

For many of these overweight women, even food is not to be enjoyed. Those who overeat the most often enjoy it the least.

The whole language of food in the diet world is one of enmity, of mortal combat between good and evil, virtue and temptation, bean sprouts and butter cookies. In the rhetoric of dieting, snacks and sweets abound everywhere, waiting in ambush, calorically armed with fattening ingredients, always ready for a sniper assault on the unwary weight watcher. For the person brainwashed by the media into thinking that excess weight is a burden of shame, the simple act of *enjoying* food is taken away. That's why fat people prefer not to eat with other people and generally feign lack of interest in food – when anyone's watching. Underfed in public so that hunger is unsatisfied, the guilty fat person waits until nobody's looking to have her way with food, furtively and with a sense of shame and guilt. And the punitive remorse that follows such secret binges is especially damaging – the self flagellation, the inner dialogues: 'You're a worthless glutton. You deserve to be fat!' It's certain that our mental and emotional attitudes affect the chemistry of our bodies: who knows what effect such attitudes have on our metabolism? Most of the small and élite group of winning losers – people who do take weight off and keep it off for good – have succeeded in making food one of many pleasures – not an enemy. Their winning approach is characterized by a positive embrace of healthy non-fattening foods rather than a negative rejection of forbidden foods. Since both sets of people work with the same two lists, OK and Not OK, at first glance the differences may not seem so readily apparent.

But there are crucial differences in the point of view here. On the one hand there's an upbeat aggressive assertion of one's right to the enjoyment of eating, a celebration of wholesome foods. Contrasted with that is the defensive self-punishing posture of the person who is perennially fending off food, who never gives herself permission to enjoy what she eats.

Please Yourself

The point to be made here is that pleasing oneself – in many ways, and on many levels – is important. The 35-Plus Woman with a weight problem should take the time to get her full measure of pleasure in as many non-fattening ways as possible, not only at home but wherever life takes her. Making the time for small pleasures – concert listening, gallery hopping, antique shopping, floating on a rubber raft or reading a trashy novel – it's your right.

And if some task must remain untended so you can make a little time for yourself, so what?

NINE

Questions and Answers About the 35-Plus Diet

Q. *How much weight should I lose?*

A. Enough to bring yourself down to a healthy and attractive size — whatever suits your age, your life style, and the way you want to feel and look. But set reasonable goals for yourself. Not everyone can look like Cher — or should want to.

From the onset of puberty, a woman's shape is sculpted from fat as well as muscle. Women have a different body composition from men because women are built for child-bearing. Our whole physiology is geared toward providing — storing — nourishment. In other words, being 'fat' compared with today's role models.

A mature woman is courting disappointment and distress if she sets her sights on achieving the boyish body contours of the sixteen-year-old models pictured in *Vogue*. You must remember that many of these girls were *born* skinny — that's one reason why they become models. And very few women entering midlife can maintain the kinds of bodies you see on *Dynasty*. If you are a glamorous actress, it is in your best interest, financial and otherwise, to expend the enormous effort it undoubtedly takes — the time and money, the extreme self-denial, even the plastic surgery — to maintain these bodies.

If you are not naturally thin, or a professional entertainer, consider carefully the costs to your health and happiness of trying to maintain a silhouette that previous generations would have regarded as emaciated. Lose enough weight to be your own best self.

Q. *What should I weigh?*

A. This is a question every patient asks. They're usually pretty shocked by my refusal to drag out the height-weight tables. I explain that this is truly an individual matter.

Not all women who are 5 feet 2 inches – or 5 feet 4 inches or 5 feet 8 inches – are going to look alike or weigh alike. Only identical twins have the same genetic make-up. And it's your genes that dictate what kind of shape you will have – just as surely as they decided your eyes would be blue.

The only one who can determine your 'correct' weight – the weight at which you look, and function best – is *you*. In fact, you probably have a pretty good idea about what that weight is right now. That's the weight that should be your 'goal', not a number decided by a chart or diet counsellor!

Actually, the Metropolitan Life Insurance weight tables have recently become more liberal, with wider revised ranges. Nevertheless, some diet groups are enslaved by rigid height-weight charts, even to the point of requiring that their members get a written excuse from their doctors to stop dieting at 135lb if their chart says 120. At Kaiser Permanente the doctors send these patients to me for evaluation before signing the 'permission' letter.

When I question these women before I write the letter, I ask them what was the last time they weighed 120lb. They usually tell me that it was in junior or senior high school!

It is simply a mistake to imagine that your 'correct' weight is what the scales registered twenty or more years ago when you were an adolescent. Your own feelings, your own ability to function are much surer guides than a height-weight table.

Q. *What about sudden weight gain?*

A. Sometimes a woman puts on a great deal of weight in a short time. A change in life style may be the cause: A busy homemaker, used to running after active children, may gain weight when she takes a job sitting at a desk all day. Or a woman with an active job may put on weight quickly when she finds herself suddenly retired. Others gain when they stop smoking or when an injury curtails an active sports life. In these circumstances it's distressingly easy to put on ten to thirty pounds in a very short period. These are the pounds we go after in short order to take off as soon as we can. The 35-Plus Diet does a very good job of this.

Q. *I plan to keep on dieting until I lose an extra ten pounds as a safety margin. Do you think that's a good idea?*

A. No, it's not. It's counterproductive – more likely to lead to weight gain than remaining a few pounds *above* your goal weight. Here's why: people sometimes diet themselves to super-skinniness because they think it will give them leeway to eat whatever they want when they go 'off' the diet. If you go back to eating the way you used to eat, you'll go back to what you used to weigh. Guaranteed!

In fact, if you've been thirty pounds or more overweight for a number of years, it's better to be a few pounds above your 'ideal' weight, because you know you can never go off your maintenance diet.

To maintain your weight loss, use Phase Three. This phase, you'll note, is similar to Phase Two of the diet, with two to three servings of fat added to each day's menu. Phase Three also gives you the weekend off (or any two days you choose) to depart from the discipline of the diet, within reason, by indulging in foods not permitted on the diet days.

But remember that the purpose of dieting is to replace bad eating habits with new, healthier ones.

Q. *Does the 35-Plus Diet ever not work?*

A. Occasionally I will come upon a patient who is not losing weight. When I question her in detail, I discover that she has been trying to lose weight faster by not eating all the food on the 35-Plus Diet. She'll tip me off by complaining that the less she eats the less she loses. And, of course, she's right!

Almost invariably I discover that the patient has unwittingly changed the ratio of food groups we set up. As a result she was eating less protein than was prescribed, and therefore more carbohydrate in relationship to protein. True, she was eating fewer calories, but as one of our subjects demonstrated on the control diet, it was possible to *gain* 1¼ pounds with a daily intake of only 950 calories! Despite a balanced low-calorie diet, she ended up weighing more than she did when she started.

Hidden fats can also wreak havoc with the diet. On top of our national fondness for sugar, we also take a great deal of excessive calories in the form of fat. Remember, fat has twice as many calories weight for weight as carbohydrates or proteins. We take most of these fats as hidden calories – in fast foods, pastries, sauces, condiments, salad dressings and the like. Since fat occurs naturally in many nutritious foods – especially meats and dairy products – extras and toppings can quickly add percentage points (and calories) to the 35-Plus Diet equation.

Q. *What about the extra-petite person under five feet?*

A. If you are a person smaller in stature, you *may* need to cut calories to 700–800 a day by reducing serving sizes by 10 to 20 per cent. It's essential, however, that you keep to the prescribed ratio of carbohydrates-proteins-fats and do not simply cut out or reduce one group or another.

Q. *Is this a good diet for everyone?*

A. I don't recommend the diet for pregnant women, nursing mothers, or anyone who is recuperating from a debilitating disease.

A woman who was at one of my classes wanted to know if her daughter could use the diet. The daughter was 2½ months pregnant, and her mother felt this diet was better balanced than what the young woman normally ate. It may well have been. Nevertheless I suggested she come to see me for a prenatal diet instead.

Q. *What about diabetics?*

A. If you are an adult-onset diabetic and not insulin-dependent, you may use the diet if you check with your doctor. I do use it in my practice, but only with the approval of the patient's physician.

Q.   *I'm trying to reduce my sodium intake. Could I use this diet?*

A.   That depends. The basic 35-Plus Diet aims to achieve diuresis (flushing out excess fluid) *without* sodium restriction. If you've been put on a sodium-restricted regimen by your doctor for medical reasons, you should get his or her advice before you make any changes. But if your doctor approves, or if you merely wish to cut salt intake for non-medical reasons, you can use the diet and simply eliminate salt or salty ingredients from the recipes.

Q.   *What about the children? Will it harm them to eat my diet dinners?*

A.   Main courses made with lean protein foods, fresh vegetables, whole grains and fruit are healthy choices for everyone, so there's no reason why your youngsters can't share your meals – with some modifications. *Growing children need more calories than you do*, and this need should be met with extra servings of bread, pasta, milk, fruit and unsaturated fats.

I see a great many pitiable youngsters who are already morbidly obese in their early teens. Most of them come from homes where the family diet is high in fat and refined sugar. If your child appears to be developing a weight problem, you should not delay seeking medical attention. *Weight loss for children and adolescents should be under medical supervision.*

Q.   *Doesn't it take time to diet? I'm too busy to prepare special recipes.*

A.   Let me tell you about one of my success stories. A strikingly attractive and very successful young woman in her thirties, an accountant with her own busy firm, came to my programme after the holidays. She could no longer fit into her smart business suits, but tax time was approaching, and she was worried about how she'd find time for her diet.

I showed her how she could do this diet with little or no cooking and also accommodate her travel needs. She called me late in April after taxes to say, 'Let me make your day, Mrs Spodnik. I've lost thirty pounds, and I feel and look wonderful.' She related she was ready for Phase Three. Phase Three also accommodates itself to busy people's lives.

Q.   *What's the difference between premenstrual and premenopausal water retention?*

A.   To put it briefly: one goes away by itself, the other does not. The cyclical ebbing and flowing of hormones in younger women can cause premenstrual syndrome. The symptoms may include cramps, headache, depression and food cravings, especially sugar cravings that cause temporary fluid retention and water weight gain before the onset of the monthly period. When the period begins, the symptoms abate, only to recur the following month. After thirty-five, however, the *general* level of female hormones begins to drop, body composition changes, insulin levels increase and the body retains more fluid. But this type of water retention, unlike the premenstrual bloating, doesn't depart at the end of the month.

Q.   *Why do I have so much trouble trimming my waist?*

A.   The thickening waistlines that some healthy, active, attractive women develop in their forties – despite regular exercise programmes – are definitely peculiar to the 35-Plus hormone syndrome. Because these women are active and fit, with generally good muscle tone, the weight literally 'settles' in the one place left where fat can accumulate. They tend to put on eight or ten pounds in the waist area, like a little paunch, and they can't lose it. Whatever they used to do doesn't work anymore. They're into fitness, looking good and feeling good. They do everything they've been told they're supposed to do – nutritionally and exercise-wise – including pasta salads instead of meat. But they have no waistline. They may even say, 'I weigh the same, but everything has slipped: I used to have a twenty-six inch waist and now it's twenty-eight or thirty. And I haven't gained an ounce. But none of my belts fit anymore!' This is all dictated by hormones. While it's true that dieting can't 'spot-reduce', this particular problem is one area where diet rather than exercise is the answer.

Q.   *What about high blood pressure – hypertension?*

A.   I have patients who have been faithful followers of the 35-Plus Diet for the past several years and with successful weight loss have been able to get off medication for hypertension. I must stress that this was under their doctor's care, not on their own. If you have high blood pressure, be sure to discuss weight control with your doctor and follow his or her advice.

Q. *My cholesterol is high, too. Can this diet help me with that?*

A. Anyone with a weight problem should have both cholesterol and triglyceride levels checked and follow her doctor's counsel about bringing blood-fat levels down to a healthy reading. Discuss weight control and this diet with your doctor. In my practice, I have found that the 35-Plus Diet succeeds in reducing cholesterol levels as well as weight for many of my patients. But your doctor should be the one to advise in your particular case.

Q. *Is it OK to eat any kind of seafood?*

A. From a weight-loss perspective, yes. Virtually all fish and seafood are relatively low in fat and calories. Even the so-called 'fat' fishes like mackerel and herring are calorie-light compared with some popular cuts of meat. Moreover, the latest word from the nutrition researchers is that the natural oil in some fish may even help lower cholesterol. But if your doctor has advised against fish for any reason, then naturally you should follow his instructions.

Q. *What about the cholesterol in shellfish?*

A. For years some shellfish was believed to be high in cholesterol, and people were told not to eat very much of it, particularly if they had high cholesterol levels. Now all that's changed. The latest word from the American Heart Association is that you should eat all kinds of seafood, but limit the use of prawns, lobster or sardines to no more than one serving per week. Clams, oysters, mussels, scallops and crab are now permissible and no longer on the limited list. Like fish, most shellfish is extremely low in fat and calories.

Q.   *Do you advise taking oestrogen?*

A.   I do not advise for or against taking oestrogen – this is a decision to be made by you and your doctor.

Q.   *Do you recommend bonemeal or dolomite as calcium supplements?*

A.   No. In fact, in my classes I usually warn people against bonemeal and dolomite; it's my understanding that they may be contaminated with lead.

Q.   *When should I take the vitamins you recommend?*

A.   Take your multivitamins/minerals with the largest meal of the day – vitamins and minerals are best absorbed in the presence of other nutrients. If you are taking Tums as a form of calcium carbonate, I do suggest splitting the four per day and taking two shortly after one meal and the other two with another meal.

Q.   *How does the 35-Plus Diet work over the long term?*

A.   Very well, if you stick to it. Keeping excess weight off permanently is the real goal of every dieter. Unfortunately, as you probably know from your own experience, virtually all diets fail. If you have lost weight and regained it, you're in the company of the majority of dieters. The failure statistics are truly depressing: only one person in twenty manages to lose weight – and keep it off for five years or more!

In my thirty years as a dietician, I've had ample opportunity to observe those statistics with many kinds of diets. They may take weight off, but they don't solve the underlying problems or aid the dieter in keeping weight off. Until this diet. This diet *works* for the 35-Plus Woman. And it equips her with the means for keeping weight off, for good.

In the first place, Phase Three solves the discouraging water-weight rebound that inevitably follows in other diet programmes. The sudden weight regain that generally results after going 'off' a diet is demoralizing and dispiriting. At this point, many people abandon weight control and efforts altogether and binge their way back to their original weight — plus a few pounds more.

Phase Three provides the successful weight loser with the tools for maintaining weight loss permanently while continuing with a normal and satisfying life that includes the enjoyment of food and food-related pleasures such as holidays, parties, travel and dining out. She can enjoy restaurants, ethnic foods and wine with dinner. Phase Three is flexible, easy to follow and undemanding. A person who enjoys cooking and food exploration can fit her interests into Phase Three. On the other hand, a person who rarely cooks and eats out often isn't burdened with dietary demands that require specially prepared meals at home. There's no need to count calories.

Equally important, in addition to weight control, Phase Three addresses other special nutritional needs and concerns of women approaching midlife. It is anti-cancer, anti-osteoporosis, anti-diabetic, anti-hypertension and anti-heart-disease.

Q. *I'm on the road nearly all the time. How can I possibly stay on a diet?*

A. It is not too difficult to stay on the diet while travelling if you'll take a few precautions.

Many fine restaurants now offer special entrées for the dieter that are free of sauces, butter or added oil. In most instances the menu will pretty accurately describe what's going to be on the plate, without a lot of seductive and mysterious descriptions of its garnish and preparation. Even fast-food restaurants are now offering salads and other alternatives to the 800-calorie double cheeseburger. Any restaurant worth its salt should be willing to prepare food to your order: substituting a green vegetable or salad for french fries or simply omitting the sauces and fattening side dishes that can be all too tempting when they're actually before you on the plate. Ask the waiter to *remove* the bread basket and butter if he brings them around. Don't be shy about making such requests. There are too many weight-conscious people out there, making similar demands, for you to feel you're out of place doing the same.

Juggle your daily carbohydrate allowances so that they can be included in the meal which will be the most difficult to plan or control. You'll want to have as many options open to you as possible.

If you're in the car a lot, take some fruit along or even pack a small insulated bag with carrot and celery sticks, diet lemonade, food for lunch. Small sealed plastic containers filled with a gel and kept in the freezer — sold at hardware and variety stores — will keep the food chilled and safe for hours without the mess of ice. You can buy individual tins of water-packed tuna and small containers of low-fat cottage cheese, either plain, or with bits of vegetable added. When you're buying and eating on the run, check the label both for ingredients and for size of the portion. If it's twice what you need and you'll be tempted to eat it all at one sitting, *throw out the extra before* you begin your meal. You're not 'keeping good food from going to waste' by dumping it on yourself when your body doesn't need it, and eating it yourself is certainly not going to help the other hungry folk in the world. Forget the 'clean plate club': you've resigned!

Airline food presents a more formidable problem. The fact that it's usually unappetizing may help you forgo the airline meal for a better meal later. Or you may be able to order a dietetic meal if you phone the airline in advance: it may not be exactly what you want but you should be spared the floury sauces and have a fair idea of what's on your plate. If the airline can't accommodate you, don't be afraid to bring along a meal from home. Try to make it a treat: vegetable nibbles, your favourite fruit, a good grilled steak chilled and sliced thin so you can roll the slices and eat them with your fingers, your favourite dill pickles. Your seat-mate will be envious.

Breakfast at a restaurant is easy: you should be able to order almost anything that you would prepare at home. But beware of filled omelettes and scrambled eggs, which the cook will prob-ably prepare with butter.

When ordering dinner, avoid fried foods, sauces and gravy. You could have lean roast beef, filet mignon, grilled fish, or roast chicken with the skin removed. You could have, with the meat, half a large baked potato with a vegetable side dish and salad. Avoid rich salad dressings, sour cream, butter, anything sweetened with sugar. Some fat may be on the grilled fish or chicken. If possible, request that it be grilled with a minimum of oil. For dessert, have fresh fruit or save your allotted drink (have a Perrier or other mineral water with lime before dinner) and have brandy and coffee instead of dessert. Avoid liqueurs, which are loaded with sugar.

TEN

Twenty-five Ways to Make Your Diet Work Better

- Don't skip meals. If you pass up breakfast, you'll only overeat at lunch – or snack mid-morning on unhealthy foods. Make breakfast the time for filling, high-fibre fruit, whole-grain cereal and calcium-rich skimmed milk.
- Take a walk before or after dinner. It's the best exercise for using calories and controlling appetite – much better than sporadic strenuous workouts.
- Always eat the most filling, least fattening foods first – salad before the meal, not after.
- Never reward yourself with food. The food pay-off habit makes you think you're hungry whenever life gives you a hard time.
- Make time to eat properly – forget the grazing craze. Gobbling and snacking on the run only leave you hungry and unsatisfied.
- Enjoy what you eat. *Focus* on your food. Savour the flavour of every morsel. Get a full measure of enjoyment from every bite.
- Shop for food after meals, not before. If you go to the supermarket hungry, you'll be tempted to buy more than you need.
- Make a careful shopping list. And don't buy any food not on it.
- When you bring home raw vegetables from the grocery store, clean and prepare them immediately. Carrot and celery sticks, broccoli and cauliflower florets will keep very well if stored, well-drained, in a big plastic bag in your refrigerator. Having

these handy is a great time-saver and you'll be particularly grateful for them if you have a sudden snack attack.

● Avoid sugar and sugar-containing foods or beverages. Sugar raises your insulin level and creates hunger.

● Satisfy your sweet tooth with fresh fruit. The natural fruit sugar in fruit is handled differently by the body. And fresh fruit contains appetite-appeasing fibre and pectin that hold moisture and create stomach-filling bulk.

● Learn to eat just one. One brownie instead of a whole batch. That's what maintenance is all about.

● Fill up on liquids. Think you're hungry? Have a big glass of iced water or a hot bowl of soup before dinner.

● Don't eat between meals. If three squares plus a snack means you find yourself tempted in between, schedule additional snacks made up of raw vegetables.

● Make sure you eat your fill of the high-fibre foods your diet permits: whole grains, fresh fruits and vegetables, beans, bran and other filling fare. They fill you up faster and help keep you feeling full longer.

● Add foods with a high water content to your menu: lettuce, most salad vegetables, many fruits (especially melons), sugarless gelatin desserts.

● Don't use food as a tranquillizer. Chewing to relieve tension is a habit that originates in infancy. If you can't beat the urge to chew, keep celery sticks handy.

● Forget about it! Try not to think, talk or read about food between meals. Avoid food ads and discussions of favourite recipes or restaurants.

● Slow down. If you're the first to finish eating, you'll be eyeing second helpings while others are finishing.

● Avoid bland and boring foods; focus on the spicy, well-seasoned foods that make an impression on your taste buds.

● Make your meals a habit: eat in the same place at the same time as often as feasible.

● Use your head! Use thought control techniques to 'turn off' the attraction of fattening foods. If you visualize a jam doughnut as glutted with artery-clogging fat and sugar, it will have less appeal.

● Avoid 'bad companions' – people and places that cause you to consume foods you shouldn't eat. If you can't walk by the bakery without the fragrance of cinnamon buns taking control of your brain, walk on the other side of the street.

● If one scoop is never enough, don't bring cartons of ice-cream into the house. When you're in maintenance and have a 'vacation day' from the diet, have your ice-cream at a café and order a single scoop. Save such splurges for food you really love.

● Keep food out of sight, wrapped in foil rather than see-through plastic.

The 35-Plus Diet Cookbook

A Note on the Recipes

The number of people the recipe will serve is indicated at the end of each recipe. Also indicated are the number of 'servings' or units from the various food groups – as defined in Chapter 3 and the 35-Plus-Diet Food Lists in Chapter 4 – that the recipe provides. These servings are calculated per portion (that is, per person served) at the end of each recipe, and the following abbreviations are used:

Fruit	FR
Grain/Starch	ST
Lean Protein	PR
Light Vegetables	VEG
Skimmed Milk/Yogurt	ML

ELEVEN.

Breakfast and Brunch Ideas

Many of the recipes in this breakfast and brunch section could also serve as lunch or supper dishes.

Two Simple Methods for Cooking Eggs Without Added Fat

Poached Eggs

Pour water into a saucepan to the height of 2in/5cm. The secret to poaching eggs successfully is to heat the water only to a simmer, *not* to a hard boil, which will break up the egg. Break each egg individually into a saucer. Tilt the saucer so that the egg slips into the water. Simmer egg for 3 to 5 minutes, depending on size. Remove with a slotted spoon.

Each egg provides: 1 PR

Scrambled Eggs

Beat 1 tablespoon water or skimmed milk into each egg. Coat a non-stick pan with cooking oil. Heat the pan over medium heat. When hot, add eggs. Use a wooden spoon or heat-proof rubber spatula to lift and move eggs gently as they cook. Continue stirring until the desired texture is reached. Remove from heat and season to taste.

Each egg provides: 1 PR

Omelette

Basic Recipe

2 eggs
2 tablespoons water
Salt and pepper to taste

Fork-blend 2 eggs with 2 tablespoons water. Season to taste with salt and pepper, if desired. Coat a small non-stick omelette pan with cooking oil. Heat the pan over medium heat. When the pan is hot, add the egg mixture. Cook 30 seconds without disturbing, then shake the pan gently. Use a spatula or heat-proof egg slice to lift the eggs so that the uncooked portion can run beneath. When eggs are set, tilt the pan and lift one edge of the cooked omelette with the spatula or egg slice. Gently roll the omelette over and out of the pan on to a warm plate.

Serves 1
Each portion (1 recipe) provides: 2 PR

One-pan Western Omelette

4 eggs
3 tablespoons water
Salt and pepper
1×8fl oz/225ml can plain tomato sauce
3 tablespoons onion finely chopped

1½oz/40g red and green pepper chopped
Optional: ½ teaspoon fresh garlic crushed
Chilli powder to taste

Coat a non-stick frying pan with cooking oil. Heat over moderate heat. When hot, add eggs beaten with water. Season to taste with salt and pepper. Cook undisturbed until eggs begin to set. Then gently lift edges of egg with a spatula allowing uncooked portion to run beneath. Continue cooking and lifting until eggs are soft-set with a moist, creamy surface. Do not overcook. With spatula, gently fold omelette over on itself, then roll out of the pan on to a heated plate. Cut in half and keep warm.

Put remaining ingredients into same skillet. Simmer uncovered 2 minutes until sauce is bubbling and thick. Pour over omelette halves and serve immediately.

Serves 2
Each portion (½ of the recipe) provides: 2 PR, 1 VEG

Variations

Mexican Cheese Omelette

Cook eggs as for Western Omelette. Just before omelette is ready to be turned out of pan sprinkle with 4 tablespoons grated mature Cheddar. Season the sauce with a pinch of cumin and oregano, if desired.

Each portion (½ of the recipe) provides: 3 PR, 1 VEG

Italian Omelette

Follow directions for Western Omelette, but omit chilli powder. Season sauce with a dash of paprika and oregano or mixed Italian seasonings.

Each portion (½ of the recipe) provides: 2 PR, 1 VEG

Italian Pizza Omelette

Follow Italian omelette directions, but just before turning omelette out of pan, sprinkle with 4 tablespoons of grated, semi-skimmed Mozzarella cheese.

Each portion (½ of the recipe) provides: 3 PR, 1 VEG.

Yogurt Omelette

6 eggs
4oz/100g plain low-fat yogurt
Salt and pepper to taste

Beat ingredients together in a bowl. Coat a non-stick frying pan with cooking oil. Cook egg mixture in pan gently over low heat, lifting the edges and letting the liquid portion run beneath to set.

Serves 4
Each portion (¼ of the recipe) provides: 1½ PR

Creole Omelette

2 ripe tomatoes, peeled and chopped
1½oz/40g each, chopped green pepper and celery
2 tablespoons chopped onion

4 tablespoons water
¼ teaspoon dried oregano
Salt and pepper, to taste
4 eggs, lightly beaten

Combine vegetables, water and oregano in a saucepan. Cover and simmer 20 minutes, stirring occasionally. (Add more water, if needed.) Season to taste with salt and pepper.

Meanwhile, prepare a 2-serving omelette: coat a non-stick frying pan with cooking oil. Heat over high heat. When pan is hot, add the eggs. As eggs begin to set, lift the edges gently, permitting unset portion to run beneath. Roll cooked omelette on to a heated plate; top with vegetable sauce. Cut in half to make 2 servings.

Serves 2
Each portion (½ of recipe) provides: 2 PR, 1 VEG

Fruit Omelette

Small unpeeled red apple, cubed
1oz/25g seedless green grapes
4 eggs, beaten

4oz/100g low-fat
Cheddar cheese, grated

Combine fruits at room temperature. Coat a 9-in/22.5cm non-stick frying pan with cooking oil. Heat pan; when hot, add eggs. As eggs begin to set, gently lift the edges allowing unset portion to run beneath. Sprinkle with cheese, then top with fruit. With a spatula, carefully fold omelette over. Turn omelette out of frying pan on to an oven-proof dish. Place in a preheated 350°F/180°C/Mark 4 oven for 10 minutes until fruit is just warmed through and cheese is melted.

Serves 2
Each portion (½ of recipe) provides: 1 PR, 1 FR

Lean Blintzes

3oz/75g flour	*Filling*
1 teaspoon salt	1½lb/600g low-fat cottage cheese
4fl oz/100ml each skimmed milk	1 egg yolk
and water	½ teaspoon salt
3 eggs plus 1 egg white	¼ teaspoon grated lemon rind

Combine flour and salt. Gradually but thoroughly stir in the milk and water., Add eggs; beat until smooth.

Coat a 6-in/15-cm non-stick frying pan with cooking oil. Pour about 2 tablespoons batter into pan. Tip and roll pan so that batter covers the bottom of pan. Cook for approximately 1 minute, until top of blintz dries. Turn blintz out of pan on to a towel, browned side down. Repeat until all batter is used.

Blend filling ingredients thoroughly. Place a spoonful of filling on each blintz. Fold in sides, then roll to make an envelope. At serving time, reheat in oven. Makes 18 blintzes. (Serve topped with Fresh Strawberry Spread [recipe page 112], if desired.)

Each portion (3 blintzes) provides: 1 ST, 4PR
Toppings: **refer to the 35-Plus-Diet Food Lists to calculate additional ingredients. Limit Fresh Strawberry Spread to 1 tablespoon.**

High-Fibre, High-Protein French Toast

1 egg	2 slices calorie-reduced bread
1 tablespoon water	(preferably high-fibre)
Optional: few drops vanilla	
extract, pinch of ground	
cinnamon and salt	

Fork-blend the egg, water and flavourings in a small, shallow bowl. Soak bread in the mixture 3 to 5 minutes, turning slices, until all the liquid is absorbed.

Heat a non-stick frying pan coated with cooking oil, over

medium heat. Cook bread slices, turning once until both sides are golden.

Serves 1
Each portion (one recipe) provides: 1 PR, 1 ST

How about a sandwich for breakfast? These toaster-easy choices feature calorie-reduced bread and calcium-rich 'light' cheeses topped with fruit instead of sugary jam or jelly. You can substitute any favourite fruit: sliced peach, apricot, apple, pear or raisins.

Light Cream Cheese and Berries on Toast

2 slices light (calorie-reduced) bread, white or wholemeal, lightly toasted
2 tablespoons light cream cheese or Yogurt Cheese (recipe page 184)

3 or 4 fresh strawberries, washed, hulled and thinly sliced
Optional: dash of ground cinnamon, low-calorie sweetener to taste

Spread 1 slice of toast with half of the light cream cheese and arrange the berries on top. Add a dash of cinnamon and low-calorie sweetener, if desired. Spread the other slice with remaining cream cheese and place over berries; cut sandwich into triangles to serve.

Variations

Substitute other fresh or partially thawed berries for the strawberries: blueberries or raspberries, for example, or thinly sliced, fresh nectarines, grapes or peeled peaches. Another good combination with the light cream cheese is ½ seedless orange, thinly sliced, 1 teaspoon raisins and a pinch of mixed spice.

Serves 1
Each portion (1 sandwich) provides: 1 PR, 1 ST, ½ FR

Farmhouse Cheese and Apple Breakfast Sandwiches

2 slices light (calorie-reduced) bread, white or wholemeal, lightly toasted
2 tablespoons fresh soft farmhouse cheese (or cottage cheese)

¼ unpeeled red or yellow eating apple, cored and thinly sliced
Optional: pinch of mixed spice and low-calorie sweetener to taste

Spread 1 slice of toast with half of the farmhouse cheese and arrange the sliced apple on top. Add a shake of spice and sweetener, if desired. Spread the other slice of toast with remaining cheese and place over fruit; cut sandwich into triangles to serve.

Each portion (1 sandwich) provides: 1 PR, 1 ST, ¼ FR

Big Apple Bagel Thins and Cheese

2 thin slices (one-half standard size) wholewheat bagel, lightly toasted
2 tablespoons fresh soft farmhouse cheese (or cottage cheese)

¼ unpeeled red or yellow eating apple, cored and thinly sliced
Optional: pinch of mixed spice and low-calorie sweetener to taste

Use fresh soft bagels, if possible. Slice each bagel into 4 thin slices; use 2 of the slices (half of a bagel) for each serving. Toast bagel slices lightly.

Spread 1 slice of toasted bagel thinly with half of the farmhouse cheese and arrange apple slices on top. Add a shake of spice and sweetener, if desired. Spread the other slice of toast with remaining cheese and place over fruit; cut sandwich into triangles to serve.

Serves 1
Each portion (1 recipe) provides: 1 PR, 1 ST, ¼ FR

Pineapple-Cheese Danish Pita Pockets

1 wholewheat mini (1oz/25g) pita bread

2½oz/60g low-fat cottage cheese

2 tablespoons well drained, juice-packed crushed pineapple

Optional: ground cinnamon and low-calorie sweetener, to taste

Toast the pita bread lightly. To serve, slice each pita bread in half to form 2 half moons. Combine remaining ingredients, mixing lightly, and divide between pita halves.

Serves 1
Each portion (1 sandwich) provides: 1 PR, 1 ST, ¼ FR

Cheese Danish and Spiced Pineapple on Crispbread

Tastes like a Danish pastry!

2 high-fibre crispbread crackers

2 tablespoons light cream cheese

1 tablespoon well drained juice-packed crushed pineapple

Optional: pinch of ground cinnamon and low-calorie sweetener, to taste

Spread each crispbread cracker with half of the light cream cheese and top with half of the crushed pineapple. Add a shake of cinnamon and low-calorie sweetener to each, if desired.

Serves 1
Each portion (1 recipe) provides: 1 PR, 1 ST, ½ FR

Berry Breakfast Cheese 'n' Crispbread

2½oz/60g low-fat cottage cheese

Optional: a few drops vanilla extract

2 high-fibre crispbread crackers

1oz/25g fresh blueberries, sliced strawberries, peaches or nectarines

Optional: ground cinnamon and low-calorie sweetener, to taste

Mix cottage cheese with vanilla, if desired. Spread each crispbread cracker with half of the cottage cheese and arrange fruit on top of each. Sprinkle lightly with cinnamon and sweetener, if desired.

Serves 1
Each portion (1 sandwich) provides: 1 PR, 1 ST, ½ FR

Cheese and Orange Spread

8oz/225g calorie-reduced cream cheese or fresh (soft) farmhouse cheese

4 tablespoons orange juice concentrate

For easiest mixing, allow both ingredients to reach room temperature, then beat together until fluffy. Store in the refrigerator. (May be sweetened with sugar substitute and spiced with a pinch of cinnamon to taste, if desired.)

Serves 4
Each portion (2 tablespoons) provides: 1 PR

Blueberry Jam

2½lb/1.25kg fresh blueberries
1 sachet plain gelatin

6fl oz/200ml apple juice concentrate
2 tablespoons lemon juice

Purée blueberries in food processor or blender, in two or three batches; set aside. Sprinkle the gelatin on half the apple juice concentrate in a small pan or microwave dish. While gelatin is softening, combine remaining apple juice concentrate with lemon juice.

When the gelatin is soft, heat gently until melted. Combine melted gelatin, fruit juice and puréed blueberries; mix well. Spoon into 8oz/225g jam jars; label and store in freezer. Keep refrigerated once opened.

Makes 10 8oz/225g jars

Variation

Blackberry Jam

For best results, combine fresh blackberries with blueberries to minimize the seediness of the blackberries. Follow preceding recipe, using 1½lb/675g blueberries and 1lb/450g fresh black-berries.

Limit servings to 1 tablespoon per day.

Fresh Strawberry Spread

8oz/225g fresh strawberries
1 package (4-serving)
sugar-free strawberry jelly
8fl oz/225ml boiling water

Wash, hull and mash the strawberries well. Stir the jelly into boiling water until completely dissolved, then combine with mashed strawberries. Refrigerate (stir once or twice) until set. Spoon into jam jars, cover and store in the refrigerator.

Makes 3 8oz/225g jars
Limit servings to 1 tablespoon per day.

Speedy Strawberry Syrup

4oz/100g low-sugar or sugarless strawberry jam or preserves (or any favourite flavour)

4fl oz/100ml water
Optional: 3 packets low-calorie sweetener

Combine jam and water in a saucepan. Cook and stir over low heat until simmering. Remove from heat and stir in sugar substitute, if desired. Serve with pancakes or French toast.

Makes 8fl oz/225ml
Limit servings to 1 tablespoon per day.

TWELVE

Lunch and Supper

These recipes are apportioned for lunch or light supper. In many instances, the size of each portion can be doubled to provide you with an entrée suitable for your main meal. Check allowances carefully, particularly for carbohydrate (ST) content to be sure that a larger portion does not exceed your carbohydrate allowance.

Middle Eastern Sloppy Joes

1lb/450g fat-trimmed lean beef topside, minced
3 medium onions, chopped
3 large sticks celery, chopped
½ green pepper, chopped
8fl oz/225ml plain tomato sauce

4 tablespoons each lemon juice and chopped fresh parsley
1 tablespoon cumin seeds
Garlic salt and pepper, to taste
4 wholewheat mini 1oz/25g pita breads with sesame seeds

Coat a large non-stick frying pan or electric frying pan with cooking oil. Spread the mince in a shallow layer and brown over high heat. When underside is done, break the meat into chunks and turn it to brown evenly. Discard any melted fat from pan. Stir in the onion; cook and stir just until onion begins to brown. Stir in celery, pepper and tomato sauce. Add lemon juice, parsley and seasonings.

Toast the pita breads lightly. To serve, slice each pita bread partially around the border, then open to form a pocket. Spoon in the spicy beef mixture and serve immediately.

Serves 4
Each portion (¼ of the recipe) provides: 3 PR, 1 ST, 1 VEG

Aegean Beefy Pita Pockets

4 grilled hamburgers
1×8oz/225g can tomatoes
1 onion, chopped
2 tablespoons fresh (or 2
teaspoons dried) mint or oregano,
chopped

Dash each ground cinnamon and
nutmeg
4×1oz/25g mini pita breads
12 dill pickle slices
4oz/100g crumbled feta cheese

Break up hamburgers; combine in a saucepan with tomatoes, onion, herbs and spices. Simmer until meat is heated through.

Split pita breads around edges and open to form pockets. Spoon the hot mixture into the pockets; add pickles and cheese.

Serves 4
Each portion (¼ of recipe) provides: 4 PR, 1 ST

Barbecue in a Pita Pocket

12fl oz/350ml plain or seasoned
tomato juice
1 tablespoon cider vinegar
6 tablespoons unsweetened
pineapple (or apple) juice
2 tablespoons Worcestershire
sauce
1 tablespoon finely chopped
onion
1 clove garlic, crushed
½ teaspoon celery seed

¼ teaspoon paprika
Pinch of ground cloves
½ to 1 teaspoon chilli powder (or
more to taste)
10oz/275g fat-trimmed, lean roast
beef or pork, minced or thinly
sliced
Optional: 2 to 3 packets low-
calorie sweetener
4 mini pita breads

Combine tomato juice, vinegar, fruit juice, Worcestershire sauce and all seasonings in a saucepan. Simmer uncovered 6 to 8 minutes, until sauce is thick. Stir in meat and heat through. Remove from heat and stir in low-calorie sweetener, if desired. Spoon meat and sauce mixture over slightly toasted, small pita breads, split to form pockets.

Serves 4
Each portion (¼ of the recipe) provides: 3 PR, 1 ST

Sloppy Joe Spaghetti Squash

1 medium spaghetti squash	1×8oz/225g can plain tomato sauce
8fl oz/225ml water	12fl oz/350ml mixed vegetable
1lb/450g minced beef	juice
1 teaspoon each oregano, basil,	½ green pepper, chopped
garlic salt, and pepper, to taste	1×4oz/100g can mushrooms,
Optional: pinch of red pepper	undrained
flakes	Optional: 4 tablespoons grated
1×1lb/450g can stewed tomatoes	Parmesan cheese

Puncture the spaghetti squash in several places with a skewer. Put the squash in a shallow roasting tin, add water, and bake it uncovered in a preheated 350°F/180°C/Gas Mark 4 oven about 45 minutes.

While squash is baking, prepare the sauce. Coat a large non-stick or electric frying pan with cooking oil. Spread the minced meat in a shallow layer; sprinkle it with herbs and seasonings. Brown the meat, with no fat added, over moderate heat. When the underside is brown, break the meat into chunks and turn the chunks over to brown evenly. Drain and discard fat from pan. Stir in remaining ingredients (except cheese). Cover and simmer 5 minutes. Uncover and simmer until sauce is thick and reduced, about 20 to 25 minutes more.

Remove the squash from the oven and slice it in half; scrape out and discard the seeds. Scrape out the yellow strands and fluff with the tines of a fork to form a vegetable spaghetti.

To serve, spoon the meat sauce over the spaghetti squash (and sprinkle with grated cheese if desired).

Serves 4
Each portion (¼ of the recipe) provides: 3½ PR, 1 VEG

Note Spaghetti squash (spaghetti marrow or vegetable spaghetti) is sometimes available from supermarkets.

One-Step Lazy Lasagne

*This version contains more protein than pasta,
and the lasagne noodles need no precooking.*

7oz/200g uncooked high-protein lasagne noodles
4fl oz/225ml boiling water
2lb/900g cottage cheese
2 beaten eggs
4 tablespoons fresh parsley, finely chopped
4 tablespoons chives (or onion), finely chopped
1 teaspoon each dried oregano and basil
Dash each garlic salt and ground nutmeg
1¼lb/500g canned tomatoes
12 thin slices (6oz/175g) semi-skimmed Mozzarella cheese
12oz/350g extra lean minced beef or veal
Dash of coarse pepper
3 tablespoons each Italian-seasoned breadcrumbs and grated Parmesan cheese

Arrange half of the uncooked noodles in a single layer in the bottom of a non-stick rectangular 9×13-inch/22.5×32.5-cm baking dish; break up the noodles to fit. Pour on the boiling water. Set aside.

Stir the cottage cheese with the eggs, parsley, chives, oregano, basil, garlic salt and nutmeg. Spread the mixture evenly over the layer of noodles. Cover with remaining noodles, arranged in a single layer, then the tomatoes, reserving the juice. Add the Mozzarella in a single layer and cover with tomato juice.

Season the minced meat to taste with garlic salt and pepper. Arrange the meat mixture in chunks on top. Sprinkle with breadcrumbs and cheese.

Cover the pan with foil and bake in a preheated 350°F/180°C/Mark 4 oven for 1 hour. Uncover and bake an additional 30 to 45 minutes, until topping is crusty. Let stand at room temperature 15 minutes before cutting.

Serves 8
Each portion (⅛ of the recipe) provides: 3 PR, 1 ST

Frozen Dinners: leftover lasagne can be divided into single servings, wrapped, labelled and frozen. Reheat in oven or microwave.

Variation

Veal-Aubergine-Cheese Casserole

Substitute 1 large aubergine, thinly sliced, for the lasagne noodles; omit the boiling water. Use minced veal in place of beef.
Reduce baking time to 1½ hours.

Each portion (⅛ of the recipe) provides: 3PR, ¼ VEG

Beef Fajitas

*Fajitas are soft flour tortillas filled with marinated lean beef
and spicy toppings.*

10oz/275g leftover roast beef
(lean only), thinly sliced
2 tablespoons lime or lemon juice
1 garlic clove, crushed
4 flour tortillas
4 slices ripe tomato

8 thin dill pickle slices
Optional: chilli sauce or Tabasco
4 tablespoons each chopped
onion, finely chopped coriander
leaves (or parsley), plain low-fat
yogurt

Combine meat in a plastic bag with lime juice and garlic.
Marinate 30 minutes at room temperature or several hours in
the refrigerator.

Wrap tortillas in foil and warm them in a 350°F/180°C/Mark 4
oven for 6 to 8 minutes. Leave them wrapped in foil.

Prepare and assemble remaining ingredients. Gently heat
beef in its marinade.

For each serving, combine sliced beef on a warm tortilla and
garnish with a slice of tomato, pickle and a tablespoon each of
chopped onion, coriander, chilli sauce, yogurt. Fold up and eat
with fingers.

Serves 4
Each portion (¼ of the recipe) provides: 3 PR, 1 ST

Variation
Fajita Pitas

Replace the flour tortillas with small 1oz/25g pita breads, lightly toasted. Split each pita at the edge to form a pocket and divide cooked lean beef and other ingredients among them.

Each portion (¼ of the recipe) provides: 3 PR, 1 ST

Skinny Skillet Chilli

1lb/450g fat-trimmed minced beef topside
1lb/450g canned kidney beans, drained
1 × 1lb/450g can tomatoes
1 × 8fl oz/225ml plain tomato sauce

2 onions, chopped
1 pepper, seeded and chopped
1 or 2 cloves garlic, crushed
1 tablespoon chilli powder (or more, to taste)

Brown beef in a non-stick frying pan with no fat added. Break into chunks and turn to brown evenly. Drain and discard fat from pan.

Stir in all remaining ingredients. Cover and simmer 20 minutes. Uncover and continue cooking until thickened.

Serves 4
Each portion (¼ of the recipe) provides: 3 PR, 1 ST

Budget Veal Cutlet

1lb/450g fat-trimmed minced veal
1 egg, beaten
Grated peel of 1 lemon
¼ teaspoon grated nutmeg

Salt (or onion salt) and pepper, to taste
6 tablespoons Italian-seasoned breadcrumbs

Coat a large non-stick frying pan with cooking oil. Combine ingredients, except breadcrumbs, and mix lightly.

Sprinkle half the breadcrumbs on a shallow plate. Shape one quarter of meat mixture into a flat 'cutlet' and press into the crumbs, lightly coating both sides. Make three or more cutlets with remaining meat mixture and breadcrumbs.

Brown the cutlets in the frying pan over moderate heat. Turn to brown other side evenly. Cook about 2 to 3 minutes per side.

Serves 4
Each portion (¼ of the recipe) provides: 3 PR, ¼ ST

Variation

Veal Cutlets Parmigiana

Follow preceding recipe. Top each serving with 4fl oz/100ml oregano-seasoned tomato sauce and a 1-oz/25-g slice of semi-skimmed Mozzarella cheese.

Each portion (¼ of the recipe) provides: 4 PR, ¼ ST

Vealburgers Paprikash

1lb/450g fat-trimmed minced veal
4oz/100g plain low-fat yogurt
2 tablespoons Worcestershire
sauce
3 tablespoons chopped onion (or

1 tablespoon dried flakes)
1 tablespoon paprika
Garlic salt and pepper, to taste
5oz/150g sliced mushrooms

Combine ingredients, except mushrooms. Shape into 4 'cutlets'. Arrange on a baking tray in a single layer; surround with mushrooms. Bake in preheated 475°F/240°C/Mark 9 oven, 8 to 10 minutes each side.

Serves 4
Each portion (¼ of the recipe) provides: 3 PR, 1 VEG

Lemon Vealburgers with Capers

2lb/900g minced veal
1 small onion, finely chopped
1 egg
4 tablespoons seasoned
breadcrumbs

Coarse black pepper
8 teaspoons drained capers
Juice of 2 lemons

Lightly mix veal, onion, egg, and breadcrumbs. Season with pepper (but omit any salt). Take half of the meat mixture and shape it into eight small patties. Flatten each patty gently. Place a teaspoon of capers in the middle of each. Sprinkle with more pepper and lemon juice.

Shape remaining meat mixture into eight more patties. Arrange these on top of the first patties, so that the capers are inside, and you have eight stuffed patties. Gently press edges of each patty together, sealing the stuffing inside. Brush lightly with additional lemon juice. Grill or barbecue 3 in/7.5cm from heat source about 4 to 5 minutes per side.

Serves 8
Each portion (⅛ of recipe) provides: 3 PR, ¼ ST

Quiche Lorraine

8oz/225g sliced ham (or streaky bacon)
6 eggs
8fl oz/225ml skimmed milk

1 onion, finely chopped
1 tablespoon chives, chopped
Dash each of nutmeg and pepper
10oz/275g low-fat cheese, grated

Coat a 9in/22.5-cm pie dish with cooking oil and arrange ham (or bacon) in dish. Beat eggs, add milk, onion, chives and seasonings. Mix well. Stir in grated cheese. Pour mixture over ham or bacon.

Bake at 325°F/170°C/Mark 3 for 35 to 45 minutes, or until a knife inserted into the centre comes out clean.

Serves 8
Each portion (⅛ of the recipe) provides: 3 PR

Polynesian Chicken Salad

About 12oz/350g diced, cooked, white-meat chicken
2 tablespoons soy sauce
8oz/225g diced celery
12oz/350g fresh (or juice-packed canned, drained) pineapple chunks
4oz/100g canned water chestnuts, sliced and drained

3 tablespoons each low-calorie mayonnaise, plain (or pineapple)
low-fat yogurt, unsweetened
pineapple juice (from canned pineapple, if you are using it)
Pinch of ground cinnamon
Lettuce

Stir chicken with soy sauce and marinate 15 to 20 minutes. Mix with remaining ingredients, except lettuce. Mound on beds of lettuce.

Serves 4
Each portion (¼ of the recipe) provides: 3 PR, 1 VEG

Oven Turkey Barbecue

2lb/900g turkey roast
1 tablespoon prepared mustard
4fl oz/100ml each red wine
vinegar, chilli sauce, light beer,
and tomato juice

Garlic salt and coarse pepper, to
taste

Thaw turkey roast if frozen. Combine remaining ingredients and pour over turkey. Roast uncovered at 350°F/180°C/Mark 4, about 1½ to 2 hours, until a meat thermometer registers 175°F/80°C. Baste occasionally.

Serves 6
Each portion (⅙ of the recipe) provides: 3 PR

Mexican Turkey Salad

1 head iceberg lettuce, shredded
4 tablespoons onion, finely
chopped
1 red (or green) pepper, diced
Optional: 1 fresh chilli pepper,
chopped (or chilli powder, to
taste)
1 ripe tomato, cubed
Optional: 4 tablespoons fresh
coriander (or parsley), chopped

12oz/350g cubed cooked turkey
roast
6 tablespoons low-calorie Italian
salad dressing
2 teaspoons cumin seed (or 1
teaspoon ground cumin)
4oz/100g each grated low-fat
Cheddar cheese, broken tortilla
chips

Toss vegetables and turkey with salad dressing. Sprinkle with cumin, cheese and tortilla chips.

Serves 4
Each portion (¼ of recipe) provides: 4 PR, 1 ST

Seafood Fried Rice

1 pint/600ml water
8oz/225g uncooked long-grain
rice
4oz/100g celery, finely chopped
2 eggs, beaten
4oz/100g lean boiled ham, cubed
1 onion, chopped

1½oz/40g sliced mushrooms
1×6oz/175g small can prawns
1×6oz/175g packet crabmeat,
defrosted
2 teaspoons ground ginger
3 shallots, sliced
Optional: light soy sauce

Heat ¾ pint/450ml water to boiling; add rice and celery. Cover; simmer 20 to 25 minutes, stirring occasionally, until liquid is absorbed.

Meanwhile, coat a light non-stick frying pan with cooking oil; add eggs. Heat gently until partly set; then break up with a fork. Remove eggs from pan and set aside.

Clean pan. Add ham. Cook with no fat added, turning occasionally, until lightly browned. Remove ham and set aside.

Add ¼ pint/150ml water to pan. Add onion; cook, stirring occasionally, until water evaporates and onion is golden. Add mushrooms, undrained prawns, crabmeat, cooked rice-celery mixture, eggs, ginger and ham. Cook and stir over medium heat until most of the liquid in the pan has evaporated. Stir in shallots at last minute. Serve with soy sauce, if desired.

Serves 6
Each portion (⅙ of the recipe) provides: 3 PR, 1 ST

Fish Fu Yung

8 beaten eggs
4oz/100g cooked seafood (flaked fish, tiny shelled shrimps, shredded crabmeat or lobster, or a mixture)
2oz/50g diagonally sliced celery
2oz/50g bean sprouts (or equivalent mixed, drained Oriental vegetables)

2 thinly sliced shallots
2 tablespoons chopped fresh coriander (or parsley) leaves
Optional: ½ teaspoon chopped fresh anise (or fennel) seeds
Fu Yung Sauce (see page 173)

Coat a large non-stick frying pan or round electric frying pan with cooking oil; preheat moderately. Add the beaten eggs. Cook undisturbed until edges of egg mixture appear set, then lift gently with a spatula to permit some of the uncooked egg to run underneath.

Sprinkle remaining ingredients, except sauce, on top. Lower heat; cover pan, and cook over low heat while you make the sauce. Keep pan covered until ready to serve. Cut the Fu Yung into four wedges, and top each serving with sauce.

Serves 4
Each portion (¼ of the recipe) provides: 3 PR, 1 VEG

Variations

In each of the following recipes, cook according to general directions under Fish Fu Yung.

Vegetable Fu Yung

8 beaten eggs
2oz/50g each sliced fresh mushrooms, raw broccoli florets, cubed raw courgettes, chopped sweet onion

4 tablespoons each diagonally sliced celery, chopped sweet pepper
2 tablespoons fresh coriander (or parsley) leaves, chopped
Fu Yung Sauce (see page 173)

Follow the preceding directions.

Each portion (¼ of the recipe) provides: 2 PR, 1 VEG

Mushroom-Beef Fu Yung

8 beaten eggs
6oz/175g rare cooked steak or leftover roast beef (lean only), thinly sliced

2oz/50g fresh mushrooms, sliced
½ small sweet onion, sliced
2 tablespoons sesame seeds
Fu Yung Sauce (see page 173)

Follow preceding directions. Cut into wedges and serve with Fu Yung Sauce.

Each portion (¼ of the recipe) provides: 3 PR, ½ VEG

Smoked Turkey Fu Yung

8 beaten eggs
6oz/175g smoked turkey (or lean cooked ham), diced
½ red and ½ green pepper, diced

3oz/75g drained juice-packed canned pineapple chunks (reserve juice)
4 tablespoons each diagonally sliced celery, shallots, sliced
Fu Yung Sauce (see page 173)

Follow preceding directions. In Fu Yung Sauce, use reserved juice from pineapple in place of part of the broth or other liquid.

Each portion (¼ of the recipe) provides: 3 PR, 1 VEG, ¼ FR

Sardines

Calories and Calcium in Sardines

3½ ounces/85g	calories	calcium in mg
in tomato sauce	196	446
in oil, drained	203	434
in brine	194	301

Sardines are named after the island of Sardinia, off the west coast of Italy. What other food can you think of where you actually eat the bones? Because these tiny fish have a skeleton as fine as a spiderweb, the bones are consumed along with the fish. As a result, a tiny can of sardines has more calcium than a large glass of milk.

Marinated Sardines

7oz/200g brine-packed sardines
8fl oz/225ml white-wine vinegar

1 tablespoon each dill seed and lemon juice
Optional: fresh dill leaves

Use sardines packed in brine rather than oil; drain well and set aside.

Heat vinegar to boiling; stir in dill seed and lemon juice. Pour mixture over sardines. When cool, refrigerate several hours or overnight. Drain well and garnish with fresh dill leaves, if you are using them. Serve on rye crackers, if desired.

Serves 4 for lunch, 8 for appetizers
For lunch, each portion (¼ of recipe) provides: 1 PR
For appetizers, each portion (⅛ of recipe) provides: ½ PR
With 3 rye crackers, add: 1 ST

Sauced Sardines

8oz/225g sardines in tomato sauce
4 tablespoons ketchup

1 tablespoon each lemon juice and prepared horseradish

Carefully remove sardines from their sauce. Combine the tomato sauce with remaining ingredients. Spoon the cocktail sauce into little cups for dipping. Arrange sardines on lettuce and garnish with cherry tomatoes, pepper rings and cucumber slices, if desired.

Serves 2 for lunch, 4 for appetizers
For lunch, each portion (½ of the recipe) provides: 1 PR
For appetizers, each portion (¼ of the recipe) provides: ½ PR

THIRTEEN

Salads and Salad Dressings

The first three recipes are for hearty, meal-sized salads. You will find additional meal-sized salad recipes under the Lunch and Supper, Main Course, and Pasta sections.

Niçoise-style Tuna Salad

10oz/275g thawed (or fresh) uncooked green beans
1 × 7oz/200g can water-packed tuna steak
1 tomato, sliced
¼ of a red onion, thinly sliced
Optional: ¼ of a red (or green) pepper, sliced
3 ripe olives, stoned and sliced

4 tablespoons olive liquid (from olive container)
2 tablespoons wine vinegar
½ teaspoon Worcestershire sauce
⅛ teaspoon garlic purée
Salt and freshly ground pepper, to taste
Optional: Cos lettuce

Combine ingredients, except lettuce. Refrigerate several hours, if possible. Serve on lettuce, if desired.

Serves 2
Each portion (½ of the recipe) provides: 2 PR, ½ VEG

Chicken Vegetable Salad

7oz/200g cooked, chilled (or canned, drained) sliced potatoes
1 × 10oz/275g package frozen sliced green beans
3oz/75g fresh (or frozen) red and green diced pepper

1 bunch chives, chopped (or ½ small onion or 1 shallot, finely chopped)
1 × 2oz/50g can sliced mushrooms, chilled
10 stoned black olives, sliced

3 tablespoons each olive liquid (from olive container) and lemon juice (or cider vinegar)
Optional: 2 tablespoons fresh parsley, finely chopped
2 teaspoons fresh (or ½ teaspoon dried) thyme
1 teaspoon each fresh basil and oregano (or 1 teaspoon dried Italian herbs)
Garlic salt and pepper, to taste
6oz/175g diced cooked white-meat chicken
1 large ripe tomato, cut in cubes (or small cherry tomatoes)

Frozen vegetables should be slightly thawed and drained; do not cook.

Place potatoes in a large plastic bowl with a tight-fitting lid. Break up and add green beans, peppers and chives. Stir in undrained mushrooms, olives, olive liquid, lemon juice, herbs and seasonings. Mix lightly. Add chicken and tomato last. Cover tightly and chill.

Serves 3
Each portion (⅓ of the recipe) provides: 1½ PR, 2 VEG, ⅓ ST

Curried Chicken Salad Veronica

3oz/75g diced cooked white-meat chicken
1oz/25g green grapes, halved
1 tablespoon snipped chives (or sliced shallots)
2 or 3 large lettuce leaves, torn
1 tablespoon each low-calorie mayonnaise and plain low-fat yogurt
2 teaspoons fresh tarragon leaves (or parsley) chopped
¼ teaspoon curry powder
Salt (or seasoned salt) and pepper, to taste
Optional: pinch of cumin seeds

Arrange chicken, grapes, and chives on top of lettuce. Stir remaining ingredients together and spoon over salad.

Serves 1
Each portion (1 recipe) provides: 2 PR, 2 VEG, 1 FR

Spiced Chickpeas

7oz/200g dried chickpeas
2 small onions, chopped
1 clove garlic, crushed
2 teaspoons whole cumin seeds
12fl oz/325ml water

12fl oz/325ml fat-skimmed
chicken broth (or additional water)
½ red (or green) pepper, diced
1 to 2 teaspoons curry powder (to
taste)
Salt and pepper, to taste
10oz/275g frozen green peas

Cover chickpeas with water and soak overnight, or boil 2 minutes and let soak 1 hour.

Combine onions, garlic and cumin seeds in a large non-stick electric frying pan that has been generously coated with cooking oil. Cook and stir uncovered until moisture evaporates and onions begin to brown. Add drained chickpeas and the liquid (water or broth or a mixture). Stir in remaining ingredients except peas. Cover and simmer until chickpeas are tender, about 2 hours.

Add green peas and cook uncovered just until peas are thawed and heated through, 6 to 8 minutes.

Serves 6
Each portion (⅙ of the recipe) provides: 1 ST

Italian Bean Salad

1 × 1lb/450g can each sliced green
beans and sliced yellow string
beans
6 tablespoons liquid from canned
green beans
1 small red (or yellow) onion, very
thinly sliced
½ red pepper, fresh or canned,
diced

4 tablespoons lemon juice (or cider
vinegar)
1 teaspoon dried oregano
Optional: 1 clove garlic, finely
crushed
Salt (or garlic salt) and coarse
pepper, to taste

Drain beans, reserving 6 tablespoons of liquid. Combine all ingredients in a glass bowl. Cover and refrigerate 2 hours or more before serving.

Serves 8
Each portion (⅛ of the recipe) provides: 1 VEG

Quick Bean Salad

1×8oz/225g can green or yellow beans, drained

1 tablespoon dried onions
Shake of dried oregano

Combine ingredients and refrigerate until dinnertime.

Serves 2
Each portion (½ of the recipe) provides: 1 VEG

Broccoli Horseradish Salad

6oz/175g raw broccoli, sliced
2 tablespoons low-calorie mayonnaise

2 teaspoons prepared white horseradish
Pepper, to taste

To prepare broccoli, trim and slice away tough outer layer of stalks. Slice inner stalks into thin chips. Break up heads into florets. Rinse in cold water; drain well and combine with remaining ingredients.

Serves 2
Each portion (½ of the recipe) provides: 2 VEG

Chilled and Ready Salad

1 head lettuce
1 small red onion
1 small cucumber

1 pepper
8 cherry tomatoes

Tear lettuce into bite-size pieces; slice onion thinly and separate into rings. Slice cucumber and dice pepper. Combine all ingredients in a big plastic bag. Refrigerate without washing.

At dinnertime, take out as much salad as you need and rinse in ice-cold water. Drain well and place in single salad bowls. Top each serving with your favourite low-calorie dressing.

Serves 4 (approximate)
Each portion (about ¼ of the recipe) provides: 2 VEG

Cucumber-Tomato Relish

2 ripe tomatoes, peeled and cubed
1 medium cucumber, peeled and
chopped
3 tablespoons each onions (or
sliced shallots) and fresh parsley,
finely chopped
1 teaspoon each fresh (or ¼
teaspoon each dried) basil, thyme,
and oregano

4 tablespoons olive liquid (from
container of olives)
3 tablespoons cider vinegar
Salt (or garlic salt) and coarse
pepper, to taste
Optional: 1 teaspoon prepared
mustard

Combine vegetables and herbs in a bowl. Combine remaining
ingredients and mix well; pour over vegetables. Cover and
refrigerate several hours to allow flavours to blend.

Serves 8
Each portion (⅛ of the recipe) provides: ¼ VEG

Low-fat mayonnaise dressing

Here are three recipes for basic low-fat mayonnaise dressings.

High-Protein Mayonnaise

1 hard-boiled egg, chopped
⅛ teaspoon celery salt
1 to 3 packets low-calorie
sweetener (optional)
1 tablespoon skimmed milk

½ teaspoon paprika
8oz/225g low-fat cottage cheese
1 tablespoon onion, finely
chopped
2 tablespoons lemon juice

Blend smooth in blender. Keep refrigerated in a covered jar.

Makes about 12 portions
Each portion (2 tablespoons) provides: ¼ PR

Slim and Tangy
Mayonnaise Dressing

8 tablespoons plain low-fat mayonnaise

5 heaped tablespoons plain low-fat yogurt

4 tablespoons each: cider vinegar, water

Garlic, onion or celery salt, coarse pepper and other seasonings, to taste

With a wire whisk, gently fold ingredients together until smooth. Add more water if a thinner dressing is desired.

Makes about 10 portions
Each portion (2 tablespoons) provides a small fraction of your allowance of milk products.

Mayogurt

Use this recipe as the base for variations below

8oz/225g plain low-fat yogurt
2 hard-boiled eggs
2 tablespoons lemon juice

1 teaspoon celery salt
½ teaspoon each mustard powder and sugar

Combine ingredients in a blender or food processor, using the steel blade. Process until smooth.

Makes about 10 portions
Each portion (2 tablespoons) provides a small fraction of your ML and PR allowances

Variations

Creamy Italian Herb

Add 1 or 2 cloves crushed garlic, 1 teaspoon each dried basil and oregano (or 1 tablespoon each of the fresh herbs).

Creamy Parmesan

Prepare Creamy Italian Herb; add 4 tablespoons grated Parmesan cheese.

Light and Creamy Russian

Add 8 tablespoons ketchup or chilli sauce.

Light and Creamy Thousand Island

Stir in 5 tablespoons chilli sauce and 4 tablespoons cucumber relish.

Green Goddess

Add 8 tablespoons finely chopped fresh parsley and 4 table-spoons chopped chives or shallots.

Creamy Garlic

Add 3 to 4 cloves crushed garlic or 2 teaspoons dried garlic.

Creamy Cucumber

Remove the seeds from half of a medium peeled cucumber and purée the cucumber in a food processor or blender. Fold the purée into the other ingredients.

Creamy Horseradish

Add 3 to 4 cloves crushed garlic or 2 teaspoons dried white horseradish.

Curry Dressing

Add 2 to 3 teaspoons curry powder and 1 teaspoon whole cumin seeds (or to taste).

Poppy Seed Dressing

Add 1 to 2 tablespoons poppy seeds.

Dill Dressing
(for coleslaw, potato or macaroni salad)

Follow recipe for Mayogurt, page 131, adding 4 tablespoons chopped fresh dill leaves (or 2 tablespoons each dill seeds and chopped parsley).

Devilish Yogurt Salad Dressing

8oz/225g plain low-fat yogurt
1 tablespoon prepared mustard
2 teaspoons lemon juice

1 clove garlic, crushed
Salt and coarse pepper, to taste

Gently fold ingredients together. Cover and store in the refrigerator. Great with pasta or potato salad.

Makes about 8 portions
Each portion (2 tablespoons) provides: ⅛ ML

Slim Vinaigrette

1 small (or ½ medium) onion, peeled
1 or 2 cloves garlic, peeled
5 tablespoons boiling water

1 to 2 tablespoons each cider (or white wine) vinegar and lemon (or lime) juice
Salt and pepper, to taste
Optional: 1 teaspoon prepared mustard

Combine ingredients in blender. Cover; blend smooth. Chill in refrigerator. Shake before using.

Makes about 6 portions
Nutrients per portion (2 tablespoons) are negligible

Gazpacho Salad Dressing

The ingredients of Spain's 'salad soup' combine to make a zesty low-calorie dressing for tossed greens.

8fl oz/225ml tomato juice
4 tablespoons olive packing liquid
1 onion, sliced
1 small red (or green) pepper, cut up

½ cucumber, peeled
4 sprigs parsley
2 cloves garlic
Salt and coarse pepper, to taste

Combine ingredients in blender or food processor; cover and process until smooth. Store in a covered jar. Shake dressing well before using. Spoon over chilled torn lettuce.

Makes about 16 portions
Nutrients per portion (2 tablespoons) are negligible

FOURTEEN

Lean Protein Main Courses: Meat, Poultry and Seafood

These recipes are apportioned for the largest meal of the day. In most instances, the size of each portion can be halved to provide you with an entrée suitable for lunch or a light supper.

Oven-Baked Beef Parmigiana

4 tablespoons Italian-seasoned breadcrumbs

4 tablespoons grated Parmesan cheese

4 'quick fry' steaks (about 1lb/450g weight in all)

1×8fl oz/225ml can plain tomato sauce

8oz/225g grated semi-skimmed Mozzarella cheese

Pinch each dried oregano, basil and garlic

Preheat oven to 475°F/240°C/Mark 9. Coat a shallow non-stick, heavy baking dish with cooking oil. Combine the breadcrumbs and cheese on a plate; press each steak into the mixture, lightly coating both sides. Arrange the steaks in a single layer on the baking dish. Bake uncovered, 8 to 10 minutes, until browned.

Pour tomato sauce over steaks. Arrange the Mozzarella on top and sprinkle with herbs. Put the baking dish back in the oven and lower heat to 350°F/180°C/Mark 4. Bake 8 to 10 minutes more, until cheese and sauce are bubbling.

Serves 4
Each portion (¼ of the recipe) provides: 5 PR, ½ ST

Aubergine Parmesan

1 large aubergine
1½lb/675g lean minced beef or veal
1×12fl oz/325ml can tomato juice
1 tablespoon fresh basil, chopped
1 teaspoon oregano
1 clove garlic, crushed

1 tablespoon onion, finely chopped
Salt and pepper to taste
8oz/225g semi-skimmed Mozzarella cheese
2 teaspoons grated Parmesan cheese

About half an hour before cooking, peel skin from aubergine and slice it. Sprinkle salt over it very lightly, then place it aside to drain.

Brown meat in greased pan, add tomato juice, basil, oregano, garlic and onion. Add pepper and salt if desired. Simmer until slightly thickened.

Coat a casserole dish with cooking oil and layer, alternately, meat sauce, drained aubergine and Mozzarella. Finish with meat sauce and sprinkle Parmesan over the top. Bake at 350°F/180°C/Mark 4 until aubergine is soft, about 35 to 45 minutes.

Serves 4
Each portion (¼ of the recipe) provides: 6 PR, 2 VEG

Italian-Style Swiss Steak

2lb/900g fat-trimmed topside in one piece
1 small onion, chopped
2oz/50g celery, chopped
½ green pepper, chopped

2½ pints/1.5 litres tomato juice
2 tablespoons lemon juice
1 clove garlic, crushed
1 teaspoon dried oregano

Coat a large non-stick or electric frying pan with cooking oil. Heat over moderate flame. Brown the meat quickly on both sides. Drain and discard any melted fat.

Place the onion, celery and peppers under the meat. Add remaining ingredients. Cover and simmer over low heat until beef is very tender, 1 hour or more. Uncover and continue to simmer until liquid evaporates into a thick sauce.

Variation

Tex-Mex-Style Swiss Steak

Add 1 tablespoon chilli powder and 2 teaspoons cumin seeds.

Serves 4
Each portion (¼ of the recipe) provides: 6 PR, 1½ VEG

Slimmer Swiss Steak

1lb/450g topside
2oz/50g celery, chopped
1×8oz/225g can tomatoes
1×4oz/100g can mushroom stems and pieces, undrained

1 teaspoon dried savory (or sage and marjoram)
½ small onion, chopped
Optional: salt (or garlic salt) and coarse pepper, to taste

Brown beef on both sides in a large non-stick flameproof casserole coated with cooking oil. Arrange the chopped onion and celery under steak. Add remaining ingredients on top. Cover and simmer until steak is tender, about 1 hour. Uncover and simmer until sauce is thick.

Serves 2
Each portion (½ of the recipe) provides: 6 PR, 1 VEG

Sauerbraten Beef Roll

2lb/900g beef skirt, thin-cut for rolling
1½ tablespoons prepared mustard
8 tablespoons plain low-fat yogurt
1½ tablespoons dried onions

3 tablespoons dried mushrooms
1½ teaspoons mixed poultry herbs
½ pint/300ml dry red wine or tomato juice

Spread beef on one side with mustard. Stir together remaining ingredients, except wine (or juice); spread over steak. Roll steak tightly; cover and refrigerate 24 to 48 hours. Pour on wine (or juice). Cover and roast in a pre-heated 350°F/180°C/Mark 4 oven, 1 hour.

Uncover and roast until meat is very tender, 30 to 45 minutes more. Baste occasionally and add more wine, juice or a little water, if needed. Slice thin to serve.

Serves 4
Each portion (¼ of the recipe) provides: 6 PR

Italian Lemon Steak

2lb/900g (about) topside
1 onion, chopped
2 cloves garlic, crushed
4fl oz/100ml each fresh
lemon juice and water

2 tablespoons each fresh
(or 2 teaspoons each dried) basil,
oregano and thyme
Salt and coarse pepper, to taste

Trim meat of all fat. Combine remaining ingredients, except salt and pepper; use as a marinade for the steak. Follow the preceding directions. Season to taste at serving time.

Serves 4
Each portion (¼ of the recipe) provides: 6 PR

Variation

Hawaiian Round Steak

Follow the preceding directions, substituting Hawaiian Marinade (see page 183) for all ingredients except meat.

Each portion (¼ of the recipe) provides: 6 PR

Baked Steak Diablo

3lb/1.5kg rump steak, at least 2
inches thick

2 tablespoons dark spicy prepared
mustard
Coarse black pepper

Trim any fringe fat from steak. Spread meat liberally on both sides with mustard and sprinkle with pepper. Puncture all over with the tines of a fork. Leave at room temperature 30 minutes.

Arrange steak on a rack in a baking dish. Put the dish in a cold oven and set the temperature to 275°F/140°C/Mark 1. Bake uncovered 2 hours, or until tender. Baste occasionally with pan juices.

Serves 6
Each portion (⅙ of the recipe) provides: 6 PR

Stir-Fried Steak and Asparagus

1lb/450g fat-trimmed rump steak
6fl oz/160ml beef broth (or water)
1lb/450g fresh asparagus diagonally sliced into 1-in/2.5-cm pieces

1 clove garlic, crushed
1 teaspoon ground ginger
1 tablespoon each cornflour, soy sauce and dry sherry or other white wine

Coat a large non-stick or electric frying pan with cooking oil. Add steak; brown on both sides over moderate heat. Transfer steak to a cutting board.

Combine broth, asparagus, garlic and ginger in the pan. Simmer uncovered, just until asparagus is tender-crunchy, 3 to 5 minutes depending on thickness.

Meanwhile, slice the steak thin (it will still be raw inside). Blend cornflour with soy sauce and wine to make a paste; stir into pan and cook until sauce simmers and thickens. Stir in the steak slices and heat through to desired taste.

Serves 2
Each portion (½ of the recipe) provides: 6 PR, 2 VEG

Carne Asada-Style Skirt Steak

4fl oz/100ml lime juice
1 to 3 teaspoons chilli powder
1 teaspoon dried oregano

¼ teaspoon garlic powder
1lb/450g (about) beef skirt

Combine juice, chilli, oregano and garlic; pour over steak. Refrigerate 1 to 2 days.

Remove steak from marinade. Grill or barbecue 2 to 4 inches/ 5 to 10cm from heat source, about 5 minutes each side, depending on thickness and desired degree of cooking. Slice very thin against the grain to serve.

Variations

Lemon Steak Italiano

Substitute lemon juice for lime juice. Omit chilli powder.

East Indian Steak

Use lime or lemon juice. Substitute curry powder for chilli powder. Use mint leaves in place of oregano.

Serves 2
Each portion (½ of the recipe) provides: 6 PR

Steak Siciliano

2 onions, diced
1 sweet red pepper, diced
1 or 2 cloves garlic, crushed
1 × 1lb/450g can tomatoes

1 × 8fl oz/225ml can plain tomato sauce
2lb/450g (about) beef skirt

Coat a large non-stick frying pan generously with cooking oil; heat. Cook onions, red pepper and garlic 2 to 3 minutes, until vegetables are soft. Add tomatoes and tomato sauce; mix well. Cook 45 minutes, or until sauce thickens.

Brush steak lightly with some of the sauce. Grill or barbecue 4in/10cm from heat source, 5 minutes. Turn meat and brush again with sauce. Grill 4 to 5 minutes longer, depending on thickness of steak and desired degree of tenderness. Slice diagonally in thin slices; serve with remaining sauce.

Serves 4
Each portion (¼ of the recipe) provides: 6 PR, 2 VEG

Hearty London Grill

2 tablespoons each dry red wine, lemon juice prepared mustard and Worcestershire sauce
2lb/900g (about) beef skirt

Combine wine, juice, mustard and Worcestershire sauce, spread over the steak. Place steak in a plastic bag; close bag and set it in a bowl. Marinate steak 1 hour at room temperature or refrigerate overnight.

Grill or barbecue steak 2 in/5cm from heat source, 4 to 5 minutes each side (or to desired tenderness). Slice thinly against the grain to serve.

Variations

Far Eastern Marinated Steak

Replace red wine with sherry or other white wine. Replace Worcestershire with soy sauce. Add 1 clove crushed garlic and 1 teaspoon ground ginger to the marinade.

Steak Iberia

Replace red wine with dry sherry or other white wine, and lemon juice with tomato juice.

Middle Eastern

Replace wine with mixed-vegetable juice. Add grated peel of 1 lemon. Omit mustard. Add 2 tablespoons fresh basil leaves (or 2 teaspoons dried basil) and 1 teaspoon ground cinnamon.

Serves 4
Each portion (¼ of the recipe) provides: 6 PR

Barbecued London Grill

3lb/1.5kg (about) thick beef skirt
4fl oz/100ml each white wine, water
3 tablespoons each lemon juice, soy sauce and Worcestershire sauce

1 tablespoon prepared mustard
Optional: 2 cloves crushed garlic and coarse black pepper

Trim meat of all fat. Put meat in a plastic bag and place bag in a shallow bowl (to catch any drippings). Combine the rest of the ingredients into a marinade and add mixture to bag. Refrigerate 24 hours. Remove meat from the marinade, and grill or barbecue 4 in/10cm from heat source until medium rare inside.

To serve, remove the meat to a cutting board and slice very thin against the grain.

Serves 6
Each portion (¹/₆ of the recipe) provides: 6 PR

Meat Tacos

Spicy but not hot, unless you top it with a hot sauce.

1 small onion, finely chopped
1 clove garlic, crushed
2 tablespoons water
1lb 2oz/475g chopped cooked
lean beef (or chicken or turkey)

4fl oz/100ml plain or spicy tomato
juice (or light beer)
1 teaspoon cumin seeds
Pinch of dried oregano
4 corn tortillas

Coat a large non-stick electric frying pan with cooking oil. Add onion, garlic and water. Cook and stir over high heat until water evaporates and onion begins to brown. Stir in meat, juice, cumin and oregano. Simmer uncovered, stirring often, until most liquid evaporates, about 10 minutes.

Meanwhile, gently heat tortillas, a few at a time, in a non-stick frying pan over moderate heat, about 20 seconds per side. Spoon meat mixture into soft tortillas and roll. Serve with Zesty Salsa (see page 173) and shredded lettuce, if desired.

Serves 4
Each portion (1 filled taco) provides: 5 PR, 1 ST

Spicy Cajun Kebabs

2lb/450g topside
Cajun Marinade (see page 183)
4 onions, quartered

4 peppers (use red, green and
yellow peppers for best effect)

Trim meat of all fat. Cut meat into 1½-inch/3-cm cubes and combine with Cajun Marinade. Refrigerate 6 to 8 hours.

At dinnertime, peel and quarter onions; separate into 'leaves'. Cut peppers into squares; discard seeds, tops and skins. Thread the cubes of meat on skewers, alternating with pieces of onion and pepper. Brush vegetables with reserved marinade. Grill or barbecue 3 to 4 in/7.5 to 10cm from heat source 12 to 14 minutes, turning once.

Serves 4
Each portion (¼ of the recipe) provides: 6 PR, 1 VEG

Spicy Sweet and Sour Meatballs

1lb/450g lean minced beef (topside)
2 tablespoons onions, finely chopped
2 tablespoons parsley, chopped
1 tablespoon prepared spicy mustard

1 clove of garlic, crushed
8fl oz/225g plain tomato sauce
6fl oz/175ml water
2 tablespoons light soy sauce
2 tablespoons lemon juice
3 packets low-calorie sweetener

Mix meat, onion, parsley, mustard and garlic thoroughly. Shape into 8 meatballs. Brown in a non-stick frying pan with no added fat. Turn to brown evenly. Drain and discard fat. Add remaining ingredients, except for sweetener.
Cover and simmer 20 to 25 minutes. Uncover and simmer until sauce is thick. Remove from heat. Stir in sweetener.

Serves 2
Each portion (½ of the recipe) provides: 6 PR

Spinach Meat Loaf

This meat loaf is good as a hot meal or as a cold lunch. For example, you can make a small pita bread sandwich of meat loaf with fresh, sliced tomato.

1lb/450g lean minced beef topside or veal (or 8oz/225g beef and 8oz/225g veal)
10oz/275g spinach, cooked, drained, chopped

1 large egg
2 tablespoons onion, finely chopped
Salt and pepper, to taste

Combine all ingredients and mould in a loaf tin. Turn meat loaf out of loaf tin into a non-stick baking dish. Bake at 350°F/180°C/Gas Mark 4 for 45 minutes. Allow to rest a few minutes before slicing.

Serves 2
Each portion (½ of the recipe) provides: 6 PR, 1 VEG

Veal Marengo

2lb/900g boneless lean veal
shoulder, trimmed of fat and cut
into 1in/2.5cm cubes
Salt and pepper to taste
4fl oz/100ml broth or stock
½ small onion, chopped

1 clove garlic, crushed
1 medium-sized green pepper,
seeded and cut into strips
1 × 1lb/450g can tomatoes, cut up
4 tablespoons dry wine

Season veal with salt and pepper. Brown in a large, oiled, heavy saucepan over medium high heat. Remove veal and set it aside.

Add broth or stock to pan. Add onion and garlic; cook until onion is tender and liquid has almost evaporated. Add pepper, tomato, wine and veal. Cover and simmer for 1 hour, stirring occasionally. Uncover and simmer 15 minutes, or until the veal is tender and sauce has thickened.

Serve hot over toast. If toast is used, one slice will add one serving of starch.

Serves 4
Each portion (¼ of the recipe) provides: 6 PR

Oven Shish Kebab

2lb/900g lean boneless leg of lamb
6oz/175g plain low-fat yogurt
1 clove garlic, crushed
½ teaspoon each dried mint and
marjoram (or oregano)

Salt and pepper, to taste
2 onions
1 red pepper, 1 green pepper

Cut lamb into 1½in/3cm cubes; discard fat. Combine with yogurt, garlic, herbs and seasoning. Refrigerate all day or overnight.

Peel and quarter onions, separate into leaves. Cut off tops of the peppers; remove skins and seeds. Cut peppers into 1½in/3cm squares. Alternate the meat cubes on skewers with onion leaves and pepper squares. Brush skewers lightly with any remaining marinade.

Suspend the skewers over the edges of a shallow baking dish. Put the dish in a pre-heated, very hot, 450°F/230°C/Mark 8 oven for 30 to 40 minutes.

Serves 4
Each portion (¼ of the recipe) provides: 6 PR, 1 VEG

Lamb Rogan Josh

1¼lb/500g cooked lamb, cut in
cubes
14oz/400g canned tomatoes
4 tablespoons raisins
½ small onion, finely chopped
1 clove garlic, crushed

1 tablespoon cornflour
1 teaspoon each (or more, to taste)
cumin, fennel seeds and curry
powder
¼ teaspoon each ground
cinnamon, ginger and allspice

Combine all ingredients in a saucepan and stir well. Cover, simmer 10 minutes. Serve with rice (3½oz/85g rice provides 1 ST).

Serves 4
Each portion (¼ of the recipe) provides: 5 PR, ¼ FR

Roast Leg of Lamb

Leg of lamb
Salt and pepper, to taste
Seasonings of your choice (some
suggestions: Middle Eastern:
lemon juice, mint, garlic,

cinnamon and nutmeg; French:
white wine, garlic, tarragon,
onion; Italian: red wine, garlic,
oregano, basil, onion)

Preheat oven to 325°F/170°C/Mark 3. Sprinkle lamb with salt, pepper and other seasonings. Place meat fat side up on a rack in an open roasting dish. Insert a meat thermometer in the meatiest part, not touching bone.

Roast uncovered with no fat added until meat reaches the desired degree of tenderness: rare: 140° to 150°F/60° to 65°C; medium: 155° to 165°F/68° to 73°C; well done: 175°F/80°C.

Remove roast from the oven and let it rest for 10 to 15 minutes before serving.

Pork Plum Kebabs

1lb/450g pork leg steak
2 tablespoons each vinegar and
soy sauce
1 tablespoon plum preserves

Optional: dash of five-spice
powder or mixed spice
4 fresh purple plums
1 onion

Slice meat into 1½in/3cm chunks; combine with vinegar, soy sauce, preserves and spice (if you are using it). Cut unpeeled plums in half and remove the stones. Cut each half into 4 thick slices. Peel and quarter the onion and separate into leaves. Alternate the meat cubes with onion and plum slices on skewers.

Grill or barbecue 3in/7.5cm from heat source about 20 to 25 minutes, turning occasionally and brushing with the marinade, until meat is cooked through.

Serves 2
Each portion (½ of the recipe) provides: 6 PR, 1 FR

Ham Steak Hawaiian

1lb/450g ready-to-eat ham steak
6oz/175g juice-packed crushed
    pineapple

Pinch of ground clove

Trim fringe fat from ham; brown in frying pan over medium heat. Turn and brown other side. Remove to a plate.

Add pineapple and clove to the pan. Cook and stir over high heat until heated through. Pour pineapple sauce over ham steak to serve.

Serves 2
Each portion (½ of the recipe) provides: 6 PR, ½ FR

Chicken and Peppers

2lb/900g chicken thighs (skin
    removed)
12fl oz/350ml tomato juice

4 tablespoons light Italian salad
    dressing
2 large onions, sliced
2 peppers, sliced

Put chicken in a non-stick frying pan over moderate heat. Cook slowly, turning frequently. Discard any melted fat from pan.

Add tomato juice and dressing. Cover and simmer 20 minutes. Uncover; add onions and peppers. Cook uncovered, about 25 minutes, stirring frequently, until chicken is tender and sauce is reduced.

Serves 4
Each portion (¼ of the recipe) provides: 5 PR, 2 VEG

Chicken Mushroom Supreme

4 boneless chicken breasts skinned
1lb/450g sliced mushrooms (fresh
or canned)

8fl oz/225ml dry sherry (or
vermouth)

Coat a large non-stick frying pan with cooking oil and add the chicken breasts in a single layer. Cook over moderate heat 4 minutes on each side. Transfer to a heated plate.

Put the mushrooms and sherry or vermouth in the pan and turn the heat high. Cook and stir until most of the wine has evaporated. Spoon the mushrooms over the chicken and serve immediately.

Serves 4
Each portion (¼ of the recipe) provides: 6 PR, 1 VEG

Breast of Chicken Cacciatore

6fl oz/175ml tomato juice
5 tablespoons dry white wine
1 large ripe tomato, peeled and
cubed
1 pepper, seeded and diced
1 small onion, thinly sliced

1 tablespoon fresh basil and/or
oregano (or 1 teaspoon dried
Italian herbs)
Salt (or garlic salt) and pepper, to
taste
4 grilled chicken breasts (skin
removed)

Combine all ingredients, except chicken, in a saucepan. Cover and simmer 15 minutes.

Meanwhile, on a cutting board, slice the chicken into cubes and discard the bones. Uncover pan and stir in the chicken. Simmer uncovered, until sauce is thick.

Serves 4
Each portion (¼ of the recipe) provides: 6 PR, ½ VEG

Chicken Cutlets with Mushrooms and Onions

2 boneless chicken breasts,
skinned (about 1lb/450g)
1 large sweet onion, halved and
sliced

5oz/150g fresh mushrooms, sliced
Pinch of grated nutmeg
Salt (or seasoned salt) and coarse
pepper, to taste

Coat a large non-stick or electric frying pan liberally with cooking oil. Add the chicken and onion slices in a shallow layer. Brown the chicken and onions with no fat added, over moderate heat for 3 to 4 minutes. Turn the chicken and stir in the mushroom slices. Cover the pan and cook over low heat 4 to 5 minutes more, just until chicken is cooked through and onions and mushrooms are tender-crunchy. Season and serve immediately; pile the onions and mushrooms on top of the chicken cutlets.

Serves 2
Each portion (½ of the recipe) provides: 6 PR , ½ VEG

Drumsticks Diablo

6 frying chicken drumsticks
3 tablespoons plain low-fat yogurt
2 tablespoons Dijon-style mustard

Salt (or seasoned salt) and pepper,
    to taste

Remove the skin from the drumsticks. Put drumsticks in a plastic bag with remaining ingredients. Shake until well coated. Or combine coating ingredients and spread thickly over drumsticks. Arrange on a rack in a roasting dish. Bake uncovered in a preheated 400°F/200°C/Mark 6 oven 35 to 40 minutes.

Serves 3
Each portion (⅓ of the recipe) provides: 6 PR

Chicken Florentine

1×10oz/275g package frozen
chopped spinach, thawed
1 teaspoon lemon juice
Salt and pepper, to taste

12oz/350g cooked, chopped
chicken or turkey
2 tablespoons grated Parmesan
cheese

Place the thawed spinach in a casserole dish that has been coated with cooking oil. Sprinkle lemon juice, salt and pepper over spinach. Cover with chicken or turkey. Sprinkle with Parmesan cheese. Bake in 350°F/180°C/Mark 4 oven about 20 minutes or until heated through and the spinach is cooked.

Serves 2
Each portion (½ of the recipe) provides: 6 PR, 1 VEG

Chicken with Pineapple Garnish

4fl oz/100ml soy sauce
1 small clove garlic, crushed
2 large skinned chicken breasts,
    split

3 pineapple rings
Parsley for garnish

Mix soy sauce and garlic; marinate chicken breasts for 2 hours in soy sauce mixture.

Place chicken on foil-lined dish coated with cooking oil. Spoon marinade over the chicken and bake, covered, for 1 hour at 350°F/180°C/Mark 4; then uncover and continue baking for 10 to 15 minutes more.

Grill pineapple. Use it, along with the parsley, to garnish.

Serves 2
Each portion (½ of the recipe) provides: 6 PR, 1 FR

Citrus Chicken Spinach Salad

10oz/275g raw spinach
12oz/350g diced cooked chicken
2 oranges, peeled, seeded and
    cubed
1 red onion, halved and thinly
    sliced

Dressing:
3 tablespoons orange juice
2 tablespoons each lemon juice
    and light soy sauce
1 teaspoon each prepared hot
    mustard, ground ginger

Wash spinach in cold water and tear into bite-size pieces. Divide between 2 salad bowls. Arrange remaining salad ingredients on top. Combine dressing ingredients in a jar, cover, shake well and pour over salads.

Serves 2
Each portion (½ of the recipe) provides: 5 PR, 1 FR, 2 VEG

Tahitian Turkey

8fl oz/225ml chicken stock
1½ teaspoons ground ginger
8 to 10lb/4 to 5kg turkey, jointed,
or 8 to 10lb/4 to 5kg turkey breasts

1×12fl oz/350ml can of orange juice
4fl oz/100ml light soy sauce

Combine chicken stock and ginger; mix well. Remove skin from turkey pieces. Coat roasting dish with cooking oil, then place turkey in it and brush with some of the stock mixture.

Bake at 375°F/190°C/Mark 5 , covered, for 1¼ hours. Turn in dish. Combine orange juice, soy sauce, and remaining stock mixture; pour over the turkey. Continue baking until turkey is done, basting often. Slice into desired portions.

6oz/175g of cooked turkey provides: 6 PR

Middle Eastern Baked Sea Steaks

1½lb/675g swordfish, salmon, or
other fish steaks
10 or 12 bay leaves
4 tablespoons lemon juice

6 tablespoons plain low-fat yogurt
Optional: fresh parsley and
chives, chopped

Arrange fish steaks on top of bay leaves in a single layer. Sprinkle with lemon juice. Bake in a preheated, very hot 450°F/230°C/Mark 8 oven, 15 to 20 minutes, only until fish flakes (don't overcook). Put fish steaks on a plate.

Discard bay leaves. Fork-blend yogurt with pan drippings. Spoon yogurt mixture over fish; sprinkle with minced parsley and chives. Serve immediately.

Serves 4
Each portion (¼ of the recipe) provides: 5 PR

Barbecued Swordfish Steaks

2 swordfish steaks (about 1lb/
450g)
Bay leaves

Juice of 2 limes
Garlic salt and pepper, to taste

If swordfish steaks are frozen, put them in a plastic bag with bay leaves, lime juice, garlic salt and pepper. Allow them to defrost slowly in the refrigerator. For fresh or thawed swordfish, put the steaks in a bag with seasoning ingredients for 30 minutes at room temperature.

To barbecue Arrange fish steaks 5in/12.5cm from heat source, and slow cook them in the smoke about 10 to 12 minutes per side. Or arrange the fish steaks in a hinged revolving rotisserie basket and barbecue them in the revolving grill about 20 minutes, just until fish starts to flake. Be very careful not to overcook the fish because it will dry out.

To grill indoors, grill 3in/7.5cm from heat source, for about 5 minutes per side. For best results, swordfish steaks should be 1in/2.5cm thick. Shorten cooking time for thinner fish. Remove bay leaves before serving.

Serves 2
Each portion (½ of the recipe) provides: 6 PR

Brook Trout with Leek and Fennel

From Adrian's Café in Philadelphia. Use this method with any small whole fish.

Fresh brook trout
Fresh leeks and fennel
Thin lemon slices

Dry white wine
Salt and pepper to taste

For each fish: Cut a circle of parchment paper (available in specialist cookware stores, or use aluminium foil) about 2 in/5cm larger than the fish. Thinly slice fresh leek and fennel (bulb part only); use about 1oz/25g of each per fish. Arrange the fish on top of the parchment and add slices of leek, fennel and lemon. Sprinkle with 1 tablespoon white wine; salt and pepper to taste.

Fold the paper over the fish and then pleat the edges. Arrange fish packets in a single layer in a baking dish. Bake for 8 minutes at 350°F/180°C/Mark 4.

Each trout (average size) provides: 6 PR

Saucy Fish Fillets

1¼lb/500g fresh fish fillets (e.g. cod, whiting)
3 tablespoons low-fat mayonnaise

1 tablespoon lemon juice
Salt and pepper, to taste

Cut fish fillets into serving pieces; combine in a plastic bag with mayonnaise and lemon juice. Close bag tightly and shake until fillets are evenly coated.

Coat a shallow non-stick baking dish with cooking oil. Arrange fish in a single layer. Sprinkle lightly with salt and pepper. Bake uncovered in a preheated, very hot 450°F/230°C/Mark 8 oven 10 to 12 minutes, depending on thickness of fillets. Fish is done when it just begins to flake; don't overcook.

Serves 4
Each portion (¼ of the recipe) provides: 5 PR

Sour Creamy Fish Fillets

1¼lb/500g fresh plaice (or other fish) fillets
1 small onion, thinly sliced
4fl oz/100ml dry white wine
6 tablespoons plain low-fat yogurt

Salt and pepper, to taste
2 tablespoons fresh dill (or parsley), chopped
Optional: paprika

Coat a non-stick baking dish with cooking oil. Cut fish fillets into 4 equal servings. Arrange the fillets over several onion slices. Pour on half the wine. Bake uncovered, in a preheated 450°F/230°C/Mark 8 oven 12 to 14 minutes, depending on thickness of the fillets. Add more wine if needed. Transfer fish to serving dish.

Add remaining wine and yogurt to baking dish and blend with fork. Spoon over fish. Sprinkle with salt, pepper, dill and paprika before serving.

Serves 2
Each portion (½ of the recipe) provides: 6 PR

Italian-Style Fish Fillets

1 small onion, finely chopped
1¼lb/500g fish fillets (sole, plaice or halibut), fresh or thawed
4 tablespoons low-fat calorie-reduced Italian-style salad dressing

2 tablespoons fresh parsley, chopped
¼ cup grated Parmesan cheese

Sprinkle onion in an ovenproof dish. Top with fillets in a single layer. Spread with dressing. Sprinkle with parsley and cheese. Cover and bake in a preheated 450°F/230°C/Mark 8 oven for 10 minutes. Uncover and bake for 4 to 6 minutes more, until browned.

Serves 2
Each portion (½ of the recipe) provides: 5 PR

Halibut in Wine

3lb/1.5kg halibut or other fish fillets

8fl oz/225ml white wine
Salt, pepper, paprika

Arrange fish fillets in an oven-to-table casserole dish. Add the wine. Sprinkle with salt and pepper to taste. Bake at 350°F/180°C/Mark 4, 10 minutes, until fish whitens. Sprinkle with paprika before serving.

Serves 6
Each portion (⅙ of the recipe) provides: 6 PR

FIFTEEN

Meal-Size Soups

Beef and Barley Soup

Meaty bones left over from beef
 roast
1 × 1¼lb/500g can Italian tomatoes
2 pints/1.25 litres water
2 teaspoons salt (or garlic salt)
1 teaspoon each: fennel seeds,
 dried oregano (or Italian
 seasoning)

4 tablespoons medium pearl
 barley
4 onions, peeled and quartered
1 carrot, sliced
1 pepper, chopped
4 tablespoons fresh (preferably
 Italian) parsley, finely chopped
Optional: sprinkle of Parmesan
 cheese

Combine meaty bones, tomatoes, water and seasonings. Cover
and simmer 1½ hours (or 30 minutes in pressure cooker) until
meat falls easily from bones.

Refrigerate until cool. Remove and discard hardened fat from
surface of soup. Remove meat from bones; discard bones.
Reheat soup and meat. Add remaining ingredients, except
cheese. Cover and simmer until barley is tender, about 45
minutes. Serve with a scant sprinkle of cheese, if desired.

Variation

Turkey and Barley Soup

Substitute meaty bones left over from roast turkey.

Serves 8
Each portion (⅛ of the recipe) provides: 1 PR, 1 VEG, ⅛ ST

Scotch Broth

Meaty bones from roast leg of
lamb
3¼ pints/1.8 litres water
2 or 3 bay leaves
Salt to taste
¼ teaspoon pepper

1 small onion, sliced
2oz/150g each sliced carrot, celery
and turnip
4 tablespoons pearl barley
½ teaspoon dried marjoram

Place meaty lamb bones in a large pot with water, bay leaves, salt and pepper. Bring to a boil; skin and discard any foam from soup. Cover and simmer 1½ hours.

Cool soup; skim and discard any fat from surface. Remove bones and dice the lamb. Discard bones and return meat to the soup along with remaining ingredients. Cover and simmer 45 minutes more, stirring occasionally. Remove bay leaves before serving.

Serves 6
Each portion (⅙ of the recipe) provides: 1 PR, ⅙ ST, ½ VEG

Turkey Scotch Broth

Meaty bones left over from roast
turkey
3¼ pints/1.8 litres water
Optional: 2 teaspoons salt
4 tablespoons medium pearl
barley

4 carrots, sliced
4 sticks celery with leaves, cut in
1¼in/3cm lengths
2 onions, peeled and quartered
4 tablespoons fresh parsley,
chopped

Combine turkey bones in a stock pot with water and salt. Cover; simmer 1½ hours (or 30 minutes in a pressure cooker) until meat falls easily from bones.

Refrigerate. When cool, remove and discard hardened fat from surface of soup. Remove meat from bones; reserve meat and discard bones. Reheat soup and meat. Add barley and vegetables. Cover and simmer until barley is tender, about 45 minutes.

Serves 8
Each portion (⅛ of the recipe) provides: 1 PR, ⅛ ST, ½ VEG

Basic Chicken Broth

Basic chicken broth can be used in soups or as cooking liquid for vegetables. (They'll taste great without adding any butter or margarine.) Use the meat for salads, sandwiches and other recipes.

1 whole frying chicken or chicken pieces	Salt, pepper and seasonings, to taste
Water, onion and celery	Optional: bay leaf, pinch of thyme

You can use whole chicken (which is cheaper) or cut-up parts (all white meat or dark, your preference). If you use whole chicken, it is not necessary to joint it, but do add the neck and giblets to the pot to flavour the broth. It is not necessary to remove the skin.

Put the chicken in a heavy casserole with a lid and add 8fl oz/ 225ml water for each 1lb/450g of chicken. Add a peeled onion and a stick of chopped celery or some celery leaves. Add 1 teaspoon salt per 1lb/450g (or to taste) and other seasonings to taste.

Cover pot tightly and simmer over low heat 45 minutes to 1 hour, until chicken is tender. Remove pot from heat and leave chicken in the broth until cool enough to handle. When chicken is cool, remove and discard skin, bones and bay leaf, if you are using it. Wrap and refrigerate meat for use in other recipes.

Strain broth and refrigerate. When cool, skim and discard the fat that forms on the surface. Refrigerate broth or, for longer storage, freeze.

Speedy Chicken Noodle Vegetable Soup

1½ pints/900ml fat-skimmed chicken broth, fresh or canned	1 small onion
4oz/100g fine egg noodles	1 stick celery
2 carrots, unpeeled	3 tablespoons fresh parsley chopped

Heat broth to boiling; add noodles a few at a time. Put vegetables through coarse shredding disc or grate coarsely, then add them to the boiling soup. Simmer 5 more minutes.

Serves 4
Each portion (¼ of the recipe) provides: 1 ST, ½ VEG

Chicken Soup Primavera

1¼ pints/750ml chicken broth, fat skimmed
2 large sticks, celery, thinly sliced
1 small sweet onion, chopped
1×10oz/275g package frozen Italian-style (or Oriental) mixed vegetables

2½oz/65g mushrooms, sliced
3 tablespoons parsley, chopped
Optional: a few fresh sage (or thyme) leaves, chopped
6oz/175g cooked chicken breast, diced

Heat broth to boiling. Add celery and onion. Simmer 5 minutes. Add remaining ingredients, except chicken. Simmer just until vegetables are crispy-crunchy, about 6 to 7 minutes more. Stir in cooked chicken and heat through.

Serves 2
Each portion (½ of the recipe) provides: 3 PR, 2 VEG

Spanish Salad Soup

1 cucumber, peeled and chopped
1 small onion, finely chopped
½ pepper, diced
16fl oz/450ml plain (or spicy) tomato juice
8fl oz/225ml mixed-vegetable juice

3 tablespoons olive liquid (from jar of olives)
2 tablespoons each lemon juice and chopped parsley (or coriander)
Optional: paprika, hot pepper and crushed garlic, to taste

Combine ingredients and chill thoroughly before serving.

Serves 6
Each portion (⅙ of the recipe) provides: 1 VEG

Minestrone Medley

1lb/450g dried lentils
2½ pints/1.5 litres fresh cold water
1×6oz/175g can tomato paste
3 sticks celery, chopped
4oz/100g cabbage, coarsely chopped
2½oz/60g mushrooms, sliced

1 onion, chopped
1 teaspoon each garlic salt and Italian herbs (or ½ teaspoon each dried oregano and basil)
Pepper to taste
Pinch of hot pepper flakes
8 tablespoons grated Parmesan cheese

Soak lentils overnight in water; drain and discard water. Combine lentils with 2½ pints/1.5 litres fresh cold water. Heat to boiling. Stir in remaining ingredients, except cheese. Cover and simmer 45 minutes. Serve sprinkled with Parmesan.

Serves 8
Each portion (⅛ of the recipe) provides: ½ PR, 1 ST

Tuna Skillet Gumbo

1lb/450g stewed tomatoes
10oz/275g frozen okra, thawed
1 onion, sliced
1 red and green pepper, diced
8fl oz/225ml water
1×6oz/175g can clam-tomato (or mixed-vegetable) juice

2 cloves garlic, crushed
¼ teaspoon dried thyme
8oz/225g uncooked long grain rice
14oz/400g water-packed tuna steak

Combine ingredients, except rice and tuna; heat to boiling. Lower heat, cover and simmer 5 minutes. Stir in rice and simmer 15 minutes more; stir occasionally.

Break tuna into large flakes and arrange on top of ingredients, along with liquid from cans. Cover and simmer just until heated through.

Serves 4
Each portion (¼ of the recipe) provides: 3½ PR, 1 ST, 1 VEG

SIXTEEN

Potatoes, Pasta and Rice

Range-Top Rice Dressing

8oz/225g raw brown rice
1 onion, chopped
4oz/100g celery, chopped
8fl oz/225ml fat-skimmed chicken or turkey broth
8fl oz/225ml boiling water
1×4oz/100g can mushroom stems and pieces, undrained

1 teaspoon poultry seasoning (or ½ teaspoon each dried sage and thyme)
Salt (or garlic salt) and pepper, to taste
4 tablespoons fresh parsley, chopped

Combine all ingredients except parsley. Cover and simmer 50 to 60 minutes in a non-stick pan. Fluff with a fork and stir in parsley just before serving. Serve with roast chicken or turkey.

Serves 8
Each portion (⅛ of the recipe, or 8 tablespoons dressing) provides: 1 ST

Rice Primavera Pronto

½ pint/300ml fat-skimmed chicken broth
2oz/50g each shredded raw carrots, courgettes and yellow squash or pumpkin (if available)

8oz/225g instant rice
3 tablespoons shallot (or onion), sliced

Combine chicken broth and shredded carrots; simmer 1 minute. Remove from heat and stir in remaining ingredients. Keep tightly covered 5 minutes or more. Fluff with a fork before serving.

Serves 6
Each portion (⅙ of the recipe) provides: 1 ST

Rice Jardin

12fl oz/350ml boiling water
8fl oz/225ml tomato (or mixed-
vegetable) juice
½ small onion, sliced
2oz/50g celery, sliced
½ pepper, chopped
1 tablespoon Worcestershire (or
soy) sauce

½ teaspoon dried tarragon (or
rosemary or mixed herbs)
8oz/225g long-grain uncooked
rice
1 × 10oz/275g packet frozen mixed
vegetables

Combine ingredients, except rice and frozen vegetables. Heat to boiling. Stir in rice; reheat to boiling. Arrange block of frozen vegetables on top. Simmer 25 to 30 minutes, until liquid is absorbed and rice is tender. Fluff with a fork to mix in vegetables.

Serves 6
Each portion (¹⁄₆ of the recipe) provides: 1 ST

Cottage Stuffed Potatoes

4 large baking potatoes
8oz/225g low-fat cottage cheese
3 tablespoons each chopped
chives (or shallots or onions),

fresh parsley, chopped,
and plain low-fat yogurt
Optional: paprika and pepper

Pierce potatoes and bake whole in a preheated 425°F/220°C/Mark 7 oven 40 to 60 minutes, or until tender, or in microwave oven according to manufacturer's directions.

Remove from oven and when cool enough to handle, slice each potato in half. Gently scoop most, but not all, of potato; combine with cheese, chives, parsley and yogurt. Mash or beat together in electric mixer bowl, or process with pulse setting of food processor, until mixture is combined. Spoon into potato shells. Arrange in a single layer on a non-stick shallow baking tray or cookie tin coated with cooking oil. Bake uncovered in a preheated 425°F/220°C/Mark 7 oven until heated through and tops are golden, about 20 minutes. Sprinkle with paprika and pepper if desired.

Serves 8
Each portion (¹⁄₈ of the recipe) provides: 1 ST, ½ PR

Potato Bake Parmesan

Small baking potatoes
Thin onion slices
Tomato juice

Oregano and basil
Garlic salt and pepper
Grated Parmesan cheese

For each potato, make several slits about ¼in/0.5cm apart, not cutting all the way through. Slip a small thin slice of onion into each slit. Combine 2 teaspoons tomato juice with a pinch of the herbs, garlic salt and pepper; spoon mixture over the potato. Wrap each potato tightly in double-thick or heavy-duty greased aluminium foil and cook 1 hour in a covered barbecue, or in the oven. Unwrap each potato packet carefully and sprinkle with 1 tablespoon Parmesan before serving. Cheese will melt.

Each portion (small baking potato) provides: ½ PR, 1 ST

Scalloped Potato Casserole

12oz/350g potatoes, thinly sliced
1½oz/40g dried mushrooms
½ onion, thinly sliced
½ pint/300ml fat-skimmed
condensed beef (or chicken)
broth, undiluted

Pinch of grated nutmeg and shake
of paprika
3 tablespoons parsley, finely
chopped

Combine ingredients, except parsley, in a covered baking dish and bake in a preheated 350°F/180°C/Mark 4 oven 45 minutes. Uncover and bake, basting occasionally, 10 to 15 minutes longer. Sprinkle with parsley before serving.

Serves 4
Each portion (¼ of the recipe) provides: 1 ST

Veggie Vermicelli

10oz/275g uncooked, thin spaghetti (vermicelli)

2oz/50g each grated raw carrot, yellow squash (if available) and courgette

Small onion, halved and sliced thin

4fl oz/100ml each fat-skimmed chicken broth and white wine

2 teaspoons fresh (or pinch dried) basil

Pinch each grated nutmeg and lemon peel

Salt (or garlic salt) and coarse pepper

4 tablespoons grated Parmesan cheese

2 tablespoons fresh parsley, finely chopped

Cook spaghetti in boiling salted water until tender, then drain. Combine carrot, yellow squash, courgette, onion, broth and wine in the pot the spaghetti was cooked in. Simmer uncovered 5 minutes. Stir in remaining ingredients, except cheese and parsley. Heat through. Sprinkle with cheese and parsley.

Serves 8
Each portion (⅛ of the recipe) provides: 1 ST, 1 VEG

Shredded Courgette with Pasta

8oz/225g cooked high-protein spaghetti (or linguine)

1 courgette

1 sweet red pepper

1 onion

4 tablespoons lemon juice

Salt (or garlic salt) and pepper, to taste

Optional: 4 tablespoons grated Parmesan

While spaghetti is cooking in boiling (salted) water according to packet directions, prepare the vegetables. Shred the courgette and red pepper by hand or with the shredding disc of a food processor (or, if you prefer, simply dice them into cubes). Cut the onion in half, then thinly slice into spaghetti-like strands.

When spaghetti is cooked, drain, then return to the same pot it was cooked in. Stir in all the other ingredients (except the Parmesan) over very low heat, just until heated through. (Or combine ingredients in a microwave-safe serving bowl and heat through at the lowest setting in the microwave oven just before serving.)

Sprinkle with additional chopped fresh herbs (and 1 table-spoon grated Parmesan per serving, if desired) just before serving.

Serve 4
Each portion (¼ of the recipe) provides: 1 ST, ½ VEG

The next seven recipes are meal-size combinations that include poultry, meat or fish.

Chicken-Macaroni Salad

6oz/175g cooked cubed white-meat chicken

1 tablespoon lemon juice (or vinegar)

2oz/50g macaroni twists, cooked and chilled

2oz/50g celery, diagonally sliced

2oz/50g carrots, sliced

1 small red onion, chopped

4 tablespoons fresh parsley, chopped

2 tablespoons fresh basil leaves, chopped

2 tablespoons low-calorie mayonnaise

4 tablespoons plain low-fat yogurt

Salt (or garlic salt) and coarse pepper

Marinate chicken chunks in lemon juice while you prepare remaining ingredients. Then, toss together lightly and chill until serving time.

Serves 1
Each portion (1 recipe) provides: 5 PR, 1 ST, 1 VEG, ⅓ ML

Cajun Chicken-Rice Casserole

12oz/350g cooked diced white-meat chicken (or turkey)

14oz/400g canned tomatoes, undrained

7oz/200g cooked brown rice

½ onion, chopped

2oz/50g celery, chopped

½ red or green sweet pepper, diced

2oz/50g yellow summer squash (if available)

1 clove garlic, crushed

¼ teaspoon each dried thyme, paprika, ground clove and allspice

Layer ingredients in casserole dish. Bake uncovered in a pre-heated 350°F/180°C/Mark 4 oven 35 to 40 minutes.

Serves 2
Each portion (½ of the recipe) provides: 5 PR, 1 ST, 2 VEG

One-Pan Chicken and Noodles with Wine and Mushrooms

Ruffled-edge noodles don't need precooking in water. They cook right in the sauce — the ruffled edges keep them from sticking together.

12oz/350g chicken (or turkey) thigh cutlets (boned, skinned dark meat)
4oz/100g tiny peeled onions, fresh or frozen
1 × 4oz/100g can mushroom stems and pieces
1 clove garlic, crushed (or pinch of garlic flakes)
1 or 2 bay leaves
½ teaspoon poultry seasoning or ¼ teaspoon each thyme and sage
6fl oz/175ml tomato (or mixed-vegetable) juice
8fl oz/225ml boiling water
8fl oz/225ml dry red wine
2oz/50g uncooked ruffled-edge curly noodles
8oz/225g fresh carrots, sliced
1 to 2 tablespoons fresh parsley, chopped

Cut the poultry into 1in/2.5cm bite-size cubes. Coat a large non-stick pot with cooking oil, add the cubes; brown over a moderate heat with no fat added.

Stir in the onions, undrained mushrooms, garlic, bay leaves and poultry seasoning or thyme and sage. Add tomato juice and water. Cover and simmer 20 to 25 minutes. Uncover; pour on wine. Place noodles on top. Arrange carrots on top of noodles and sprinkle with parsley. Cover tightly and simmer 12 to 15 minutes more.

To serve, arrange carrots on a platter or individual plates. Then stir noodles into the chicken-mushroom-wine mixture, place next to carrots. Remove bay leaves.

Serves 2
Each portion (½ of the recipe) provides: 5 PR, 1 ST, 2 VEG

Turkey Canelloni

1lb/450g minced raw turkey
1 egg
Garlic salt and pepper, to taste
1 teaspoon pizza herbs, divided
6 uncooked canelloni shells
1 × 1lb/450g can tomatoes broken up, undrained
1 × 4oz/100g can mushrooms, undrained
4fl oz/100ml white wine
3 tablespoons onion, finely chopped
1 clove garlic, crushed

Mix turkey, egg, garlic salt, pepper and ½ teaspoon herbs. Stuff mixture into canelloni shells. Place in a single layer in a non-stick baking dish.

Combine remaining ingredients and add remaining ½ teaspoon herbs. Pour over canelloni. Cover with foil; bake 2 hours at 300°F/150°C/Mark 2.

Serves 6
Each portion (⅙ of the recipe) provides: 2 PR, 1 ST, 1 VEG

One-Pan Beef Noodle Stroganoff

12oz/350g fat-trimmed minced beef topside
¾ pint/450ml tomato juice
1 × ½ pint/300ml can condensed beef broth, fat-skimmed
1 × 4oz/100g can mushrooms, undrained
1 large onion, thinly sliced
1 teaspoon prepared mustard
Dash of Worcestershire sauce
Salt or garlic salt and pepper, to taste
6oz/175g uncooked ruffle-edged noodles
4oz/100g plain low-fat yogurt
Optional: 4 tablespoons fresh parsley, chopped

Coat a non-stick frying pan with cooking oil. Brown beef, breaking into chunks and turning to brown evenly. Drain and discard any fat from the pan.

Add tomato juice, broth, mushrooms, onion and seasonings. Heat to boiling. Add noodles, a few at a time. Cover, reduce heat and simmer until most of the liquid evaporates.

Top each serving with a dollop of yogurt and a sprinkle of parsley.

Serves 4
Each portion (¼ of the recipe) provides: 2½ PR, 1 ST

Linguine with Seafood Sauce

1lb/450g firm-fleshed fish fillets (monkfish, for example)
6oz/175g uncooked linguine/ spaghetti
2½oz/65g fresh mushrooms, sliced
1 small onion, sliced
4fl oz/100ml dry white wine
Pepper
4oz/100g plain low-fat yogurt
4 tablespoons fresh dill (or parsley), chopped
16 tiny cherry tomatoes
4oz/100g raw courgette, cubed

Cut fillets into bite-size cubes; set aside. Cook linguine in boiling water (salted, if desired).

Meanwhile, coat a non-stick frying pan with cooking oil. Brown the mushrooms with no fat added. Stir in the onion, wine and pepper. Cover and simmer over low heat 3 to 4 minutes. Add the fish cubes. Simmer 2 minutes. Remove from the heat and set aside.

Drain linguine; return it to the pan it was cooked in. Stir in yogurt, fish mixture, dill, tomatoes and courgette. Mix lightly and serve immediately.

Serves 4
Each portion (¼ of the recipe) provides: 2 PR, 1 ST, 1 VEG

Southern Fish and Potato Stew

½ cup cubed lean ham (or lean back bacon)
1 large onion, chopped
1¾lb/800g canned tomatoes
2 large raw potatoes, diced
8fl oz/225ml boiling water

2 tablespoons each lemon juice and Worcestershire sauce
½ teaspoon dried thyme
Dash of Tabasco
1½lb/675g firm fish fillets

Coat a non-stick pan with cooking oil; brown ham with no fat added. Add onion; cook until tender. Add remaining ingredients, except fish. Cover and simmer for 30 minutes.

Cut fish into 1in/2.5cm pieces. Add to pan; cover and simmer just until fish turns opaque, 4 to 6 minutes longer, depending on the kind of fish.

Serves 4
Each portion (¼ of the recipe) provides: 5 PR, 1 ST

SEVENTEEN

Vegetables

Fresh, frozen or canned — steamed, simmered or stir-fried — solo or sauced — hot or cold — green beans are a versatile addition to any low-calorie meal.

Green Beans with Bacon

4oz/100g streaky bacon diced
1lb/450g fresh green beans,
trimmed, sliced diagonally
½ small onion, thinly sliced

4 tablespoons water
Salt and freshly ground pepper,
to taste

Coat a non-stick saucepan lightly with cooking oil. Cook bacon over moderate heat, stirring until lightly browned. Remove from pan; set aside.

Combine beans, onion and water in the saucepan. Cover; cook until beans are tender-crisp, about 12 minutes. Drain and season to taste. Lightly stir in bacon.

Serves 4
Each portion (¼ of the recipe) provides: 1 PR, 1 VEG

Greek-Style Green Beans

1 × 1lb/450g can tomatoes
4fl oz/100ml water
2 onions, finely chopped
3 tablespoons fresh parsley,
chopped
1 clove garlic, crushed
1 tablespoon fresh (or 1 teaspoon
dried) mint, chopped

2 teaspoons oregano or Italian
seasoning
Salt and freshly ground pepper,
to taste
1½lb/675g fresh (or 1¼lb/500g
frozen) green beans

Break up tomatoes with a fork. Combine undrained tomatoes with remaining ingredients, except green beans, in a saucepan. Cover; simmer 10 minutes, stirring frequently.

Meanwhile, wash, top and tail, and cut up fresh beans (or allow frozen beans to defrost). Add to pot and simmer uncovered, stirring frequently, until beans are tender and sauce is thick.

Serves 8
Each portion (⅛ of the recipe) provides: 1 VEG

Marinated Green Bean Medley

1 × 1lb/450g packet green beans, thawed
1 small onion, chopped
1 red pepper, diced
4 black (or green) olives, sliced

6 tablespoons olive liquid (from olive container)
3 tablespoons vinegar
Garlic salt, black pepper, cayenne pepper and oregano (or Italian seasoning), to taste

Combine ingredients in a glass bowl; season to taste. Cover and chill several hours in refrigerator before serving.

Serves 4
Each portion (¼ of the recipe) provides: 1 VEG

Minty Carrots

10oz/275g frozen carrots, thawed
5 or 6 mint leaves, fresh or dried

2 tablespoons fruit juice (apple, orange, etc.)
Salt and coarse pepper, to taste

Combine ingredients in a greased heavy-duty or double-thick foil packet and cook on the grill 20 to 25 minutes.

Serves 2
Each portion (½ of the recipe) provides: 1 VEG

Bayou Cauliflower

1 × 1lb/450g can sliced, stewed
tomatoes
½ pepper, chopped
1 small onion, chopped
2oz/50g celery, chopped
3 tablespoons parsley, chopped

1 clove garlic, crushed
¼ teaspoon each dried thyme and
marjoram, ground clove, allspice
and cayenne pepper
1 × 1¼lb/500g bag frozen
cauliflower

Combine ingredients except cauliflower. Simmer uncovered 20 minutes. Add cauliflower and cook until tender-crunchy.

Serves 5
Each portion (⅕ of the recipe) provides: 2 VEG

Courgette and Carrot Medley

1lb/450g each carrots and
courgettes

8fl oz/225ml water
Salt and coarse pepper, to taste

Peel or scrub carrots and cut into ⅛in/3mm slices. Slice unpeeled courgettes and set aside. Simmer carrots in water, covered, for 10 minutes. Add courgettes and simmer 5 minutes more. Season to taste.

Serves 4
Each portion (¼ of the recipe) provides: 1 VEG

Summer Squash, Turkish-Style

Note: if summer squash is not obtainable, try this recipe with courgette or marrow instead.

2 yellow squash, sliced
1 small onion, sliced
3 or 4 bay leaves

1 tablespoon lemon juice
Salt (or garlic salt) and coarse
pepper, to taste

Coat a sheet of heavy-duty or double-thick aluminium foil with cooking oil. Mix ingredients together well and arrange on the foil. Close packet and cook on the grill 20 to 25 minutes. Remove bay leaves before serving.

Serves 4
Each portion (¼ of the recipe) provides: 1 VEG

Cheesy Spaghetti Squash

1 cooked spaghetti squash (see page 115)

4 tablespoons fresh parsley, finely chopped

4 tablespoons each grated Parmesan and pecorino cheese

Onion salt and coarse black pepper, to taste

Toss ingredients together lightly and serve immediately.

Serves 4
Each portion (¼ of the recipe) provides: 1 PR, 2 VEG

Ratatouille with Eggs

6fl oz/175ml stock
1 medium red pepper, sliced
1 medium green pepper, sliced
1 large onion, sliced
1 clove of garlic, crushed
2 medium or 1 large courgette, sliced ½in/1cm thick
1 small aubergine, cut into 1in/ 2.5cm cubes

1 × 1lb/450g can tomatoes drained and cut into cubes, or 4 fresh tomatoes, cubed
1 teaspoon mixed Italian herbs
½ teaspoon salt
Pepper
3 tablespoons Parmesan cheese, grated
4 eggs

Pour the stock into a large non-stick frying pan and heat slightly. Put in peppers, onion and garlic; cook until stock is almost gone. Add courgette and aubergine. Cover and cook 20 minutes, stirring occasionally.

Uncover, add tomatoes, herbs, salt and pepper; cook 10 more minutes. Sprinkle on cheese. With the back of a spoon, make depressions in the mixture and break an egg into each depression. Cover, cook 5 to 7 more minutes or until the desired consistency of the egg is reached. Serve immediately.

Serves 4
Each portion (¼ of the recipe) provides: 2 PR, 2 VEG

Grilled Oriental Vegetables

10oz/275g frozen mixed Oriental vegetables
1 tablespoon light soy sauce

¼ teaspoon ground ginger
Pinch of fennel seeds (or five-spice powder)

Coat a sheet of heavy-duty or double-thick foil well with cooking oil. Add the frozen vegetables and remaining ingredients. Wrap tightly. Cook on grill 15 to 20 minutes (or 10 to 12 minutes, if packet has been allowed to thaw).

Variation

Grilled Italian Vegetables

Substitute bottled low-calorie Italian seasoned salad dressing for the soy; omit ginger.

Serves 2
Each portion (½ of the recipe) provides: 1 VEG

Vegetable Confetti

8oz/225g raw carrots, grated
1 small onion, halved, sliced thin
3 tablespoons water (or chicken broth)

8oz/225g each julienned courgettes and yellow squash (if available)
Salt and coarse pepper, to taste

Combine carrots, onion, and water (or chicken broth) in a non-stick frying pan which has been coated with cooking oil. Cover and cook 4 to 5 minutes. Stir in remaining ingredients. Cook and stir 1 to 2 minutes, uncovered.

Serves 6
Each portion (⅙ of the recipe) provides: 1 VEG

Vegetable Kebabs

1 medium courgette quartered and cut into 1in/2.5cm pieces
1 medium yellow squash, quartered and cut into 1in/2.5cm pieces (if available)

1 red or green pepper, seeded and cut into chunks
4 small onions
3 tablespoons light (low-calorie) Italian-style salad dressing
Garlic salt and pepper, to taste

Thread skewers, alternating courgette, squash, pepper chunks and whole onions. Brush with salad dressing. Season to taste with garlic salt and pepper. Grill or barbecue 2in/5cm from heat source for about 8 minutes, turning frequently.

Serves 8
Each portion (⅛ of the recipe) provides: 1 VEG

Golden Apple Sauerkraut

1 yellow (Golden Delicious) apple
1 onion
1 × 1¾lb/800g can sauerkraut

2 tablespoons caraway seeds
4fl oz/100ml white wine (or cider)

Grate the unpeeled apple by hand or with the shredding disc of a food processor. Chop the onion. Combine them with remaining ingredients. Cover and simmer 1 hour.

Serves 8
Each portion (⅛ of the recipe) provides: 1 VEG

EIGHTEEN

Sauces and Marinades

Fu Yung Sauce

8fl oz/225ml fat-skimmed stock
(chicken, turkey, beef, onion,
clam broth, etc.)
4 tablespoons dry sherry (or
additional stock)

3 tablespoons light soy sauce
1 tablespoon cornflour
¼ teaspoon ground ginger
Optional: 1 clove garlic, crushed

Combine ingredients in a saucepan. Cook and stir over moderate heat until mixture simmers, thickens and clears slightly.

Serves 4
Each portion (¼ of the recipe) provides a small fraction of your PR allowance.

Zesty Salsa

6 tablespoons crushed fresh hot
peppers, rinsed or not (or ½
diced sweet pepper)
2 ripe tomatoes, peeled and cubed
1 onion, finely chopped

1 or 2 cloves garlic, chopped
5 or 6 tablespoons fresh coriander
leaves, chopped
Juice of 1 lime
Salt and pepper, to taste

For the hottest sauce, use whole hot chilli peppers, including the seeds. Crush fine, then add to remaining ingredients. However, if you prefer to reduce the heat, use only the pepper part and discard the seeds. To tame the fire even more, chop the chilli pepper and rinse it in cold water for several minutes before combining it with the remaining ingredients. For no heat at all, substitute chopped sweet pepper.

Combine ingredients and store in the refrigerator. Serve this tasty salsa on anything mild and low-calorie – try it on a baked potato!

Makes about 16 portions

Each portion (2 tablespoons) provides a small fraction of your VEG allowance.

Sauce for Pitaburgers

Good on chicken and fish, too.

2oz/50g cucumber, diced or chopped
6 tablespoons plain low-fat yogurt
2 tablespoons lemon juice
2 tablespoons fresh (or 2 teaspoons dried) mint or marjoram, chopped

Dash each dried oregano, ground nutmeg and cinnamon
Garlic salt and coarse pepper, to taste

Combine ingredients and refrigerate until serving time.

Serve with grilled or barbecued very lean minced beef patties that have been basted with lemon juice. Pack each patty into a mini pita pocket with a slice of tomato and a generous amount of sauce.

Makes 4 portions

Each portion of sauce provides a small fraction of your VEG and ML allowances.

Coriander Sauce

6fl oz/175ml undiluted chicken broth, fat-skimmed
2 to 3 tablespoons wine vinegar
1oz/25g each fresh coriander and parsley

2 to 4 cloves garlic
½ teaspoon ground cumin
Optional: 1 tablespoon sweet (or hot) pepper, chopped

Heat broth and vinegar to boiling. Chop remaining ingredients fine and stir in. Or pour hot mixture over remaining ingredients in blender or food processor and process until chopped.

Spoon over baked potatoes, hot drained pasta, plain cooked

rice or grilled chicken. To make a sauce for poached seafood, substitute the poaching liquid for the chicken broth.

Serves 6
Each portion ($\frac{1}{6}$ of the recipe – sauce alone) provides a small fraction of your VEG allowance.

Cucumber Sauce for Seafood

Use instead of high-fat, high-salt tartar sauce.

2oz/50g cucumber (grated or chopped)
8 tablespoons light mayonnaise
2 tablespoons each, fresh dill (or parsley) and chives (or onion), chopped

2 teaspoons prepared mustard
Coarse pepper (or lemon pepper), to taste

Squeeze or press moisture out of cucumber, then combine it with remaining ingredients. Store in refrigerator.

Makes 16 servings
Limit servings to 1 tablespoon per day.

Meatless Italian Sauce

2¼ pints/1.4 litres tomato juice
4 tablespoons onion, finely chopped
1 × 1lb/450g can of sliced mushrooms (or use two 8oz/225g cans)

2 red peppers, diced
2 teaspoons sweet basil
2 teaspoons oregano
1 clove garlic, crushed
4 beef stock cubes

Combine all ingredients in a large, heavy pot. Simmer until thick. You may adjust seasoning for salt and pepper when completed. Use on cooked vegetables or meat.

This sauce freezes well.

Mint Sauce

4fl oz/100ml boiling fat-skimmed
chicken broth
Large handful fresh mint leaves,
chopped

Juice of 1 lemon
1 clove garlic
Pinch of grated nutmeg
Salt and coarse pepper, to taste

Process ingredients in blender or food processor; toss with hot drained green pasta, cooked brown rice, steamed vegetables, fish or chicken.

Variation

Creamy Mint Sauce

Substitute plain low-fat yogurt for the chicken broth. Do not cook the yogurt; simply allow it to warm to room temperature.

Serves 4
Each portion (¼ of the recipe – sauce alone) provides a small fraction of your protein allowance.

Whipped Cottage Cheese

For toppings, dips and other fresh uses, cottage cheese whipped fluffy-smooth in the food processor or blender makes a superior stand-in for sour cream. Its taste and texture are more sour-creamy than yogurt.

Choose a small-curd type of cottage cheese for more tartness, or a mild-flavoured large-curd style to vary the flavour. A bit of lemon juice can make it more tangy. Vary the texture by adding a little milk as you process or blend. Add buttermilk for an authentic sour-cream taste. The amount of milk, lemon juice or buttermilk you add depends on the moisture content of the cottage cheese. Process uncreamed or dry curd cheese with 6 to 8 tablespoons of milk or other liquid. Very wet varieties of cottage cheese may not need any added liquid at all.

Each portion (2½ tablespoons) provides: ½ PR

Lean Cream Sauce Base

6oz/175g plain low-fat yogurt
2 tablespoons cornflour

Fork-blend ingredients until smooth. Using a wire whisk, gently stir the yogurt mixture into fat-skimmed meat drippings, soups, or the cooking water in which vegetables have been cooked, to thicken and make a sauce. Heat gently, stirring with the whisk, just until heated through and thickened. Season to taste if desired. If sauce is too thick, thin with a little hot water.

Makes 4 portions
Each portion provides: ⅛ ML, ¼ ST

The next ten sauces provide a variety of interesting meatless toppings for pasta.

Primavera Sauce

4oz/100g aubergine, peeled and diced
4oz/100g courgette, unpeeled and sliced
1 onion, sliced
1 green pepper, seeded and sliced

1 large ripe tomato, peeled and cubed
16fl oz/¾ pint tomato juice
Optional: 1 clove garlic, crushed
¼ teaspoon each dried thyme and basil

Combine ingredients in a saucepan or frying pan. Cover and simmer 10 minutes.

Uncover and continue simmering about 5 minutes, stirring often, until sauce thickens and vegetables are tender but still crisp. (Add a little water if needed.) Spoon immediately over hot drained wholewheat or protein-enriched pasta (allow 2oz/50g pasta for each serving).

Serves 4
Each portion (¼ of the recipe) provides: 1 VEG
With 2oz/50g cooked pasta added: 1 ST

Sauce au Jardin

8fl oz/225ml fat-skimmed chicken broth
2 sliced sweet onions
2oz/50g each celery, finely chopped and carrots, thinly sliced
Optional: garlic, fresh basil and oregano leaves

4oz/100g courgette, cubed
½ each red and green pepper, diced
6 tiny cherry tomatoes
4 tablespoons each fresh parsley, chopped
Parmesan cheese, grated

Combine chicken broth with onion, celery and carrots. If desired, add garlic, and 1 tablespoon each chopped fresh (or 1 teaspoon each dried) basil and oregano. Cover and simmer 10 minutes. Add courgettes and peppers, simmer 5 minutes more. Add cherry tomatoes and heat through. Spoon over hot drained pasta and sprinkle with parsley and Parmesan.

Serves 6
Each portion (⅙ of the recipe) provides: 1½ VEG
With 2oz/50g cooked pasta add: 1 ST

Salsa Margarita

3 medium (or 2 large) ripe tomatoes
2 cloves garlic
1 tablespoon olive packing liquid
Salt and coarse pepper, to taste

4 tablespoons fresh basil (or parsley), chopped
4oz/100g semi-skimmed Mozzarella cheese, grated

Peel and dice tomatoes; set aside. Crush garlic and combine with olive liquid in a non-stick pan. Heat until garlic softens. Stir in tomato and seasonings. Lower heat; warm just until heated through. Spoon over hot drained spaghetti; top with chopped basil and Mozzarella.

Serves 4
Each portion (¼ of the recipe) provides: 1 PR, ½ VEG
With 2oz/50g of cooked pasta, add: 1 ST

Italian Garden Sauce

1 × ½ pint/300ml can condensed
chicken broth, fat-skimmed
1¼lb/500g frozen mixed Italian-
style vegetables
Optional: 1 teaspoon dried
oregano

¼ teaspoon nutmeg, grated
12fl oz/350ml skimmed milk
2 tablespoons flour
Salt and pepper, to taste
4 tablespoons Parmesan cheese,
grated

In a large non-stick or electric frying pan, heat broth to boiling over high heat. Add vegetables, oregano if you are using it, and nutmeg; simmer uncovered, stirring frequently until nearly all liquid evaporates.

Blend together the milk and flour until smooth, then stir into the pan. Simmer and stir 3 to 4 minutes, until thickened. Season to taste. Sprinkle with cheese.

Serves 6
Each portion (⅙ of the recipe) provides: ¼ ML, 1 VEG
With 2oz/50g cooked pasta add: 1 ST

Speedy Tomato and Mushroom Sauce

8fl oz/225ml each plain tomato
sauce and dry white wine
7oz/200g undrained canned
tomatoes

2½oz/60g mushroom stems and
pieces
1 teaspoon each dried oregano
and thyme
Optional: 1 clove garlic, crushed

Combine ingredients in a saucepan and simmer uncovered 20 to 25 minutes until sauce is reduced and thick. Spoon over pasta.

Serves 6
Each portion (⅙ of the recipe) provides: 1 VEG
With 2oz/50g cooked pasta, add: 1 ST

Basil Sauce

6fl oz/175ml boiling water or fat-
skimmed chicken broth
1 large handful fresh basil leaves
3 cloves garlic

4 tablespoons Parmesan cheese,
grated
Salt and pepper, to taste

Combine ingredients in blender or food processor and process until basil and garlic are crushed. Or process by hand, using a mortar and pestle to mash basil and garlic together, then mix with remaining ingredients.

Add the sauce to hot drained pasta and toss lightly.

Serves 4
Each portion (¼ of the recipe) provides a small fraction of your protein allowance.
With 2oz/50g cooked pasta, add: 1 ST

Pesto Sauce

1lb/450g low-fat cottage (or skimmed milk ricotta) cheese
2 large cloves garlic, peeled
2 large handfuls each, fresh parsley and basil (or raw spinach)
8fl oz/225ml boiling water

10 tablespoons Parmesan (or pecorino) cheese, grated
Salt and coarse pepper, to taste
12oz/350g spaghetti, cooked until tender

Have cheese at room temperature. Combine with remaining ingredients, except spaghetti, in blender (or food processor, using steel blade). Cover; blend smooth. Toss with hot drained spaghetti.

Serves 6
Each portion (⅙ of the recipe, including pasta) provides: 2 PR, 1 ST

Spinach Ricotta Sauce

8oz/225g semi-skimmed ricotta cheese
1 clove garlic

1oz/25g raw spinach leaves
Grated nutmeg, lemon peel, salt, pepper

Have ricotta at room temperature. Combine with garlic and spinach in food processor, using the steel blade. Process until completely smooth; season to taste. Toss with hot drained pasta.

Serves 6
Each portion (⅙ of the recipe) provides: 1 PR, ⅓ VEG
With 2oz/50g cooked pasta add: 1 ST

Italian Pepper Sauce

1 tablespoon olive packing liquid
1 onion, finely chopped
1 clove garlic, crushed
8fl oz/225ml fat-skimmed chicken broth

3 green (or red) peppers, diced or grated
2 tablespoons each fresh basil and parsley, chopped
Optional: Salt and coarse pepper, to taste

Coat a non-stick frying pan with cooking oil. Add olive liquid, onion and garlic; cook and stir 2 minutes. Add remaining ingredients; cover and simmer 7 to 8 minutes. Toss with hot drained pasta.

Serves 4
Each portion (¼ of the recipe) provides: 1 VEG
With 2oz/50g cooked pasta, add: 1 ST

Piedmont Parsley Sauce

8fl oz/225ml fat-skimmed hot chicken broth
1 to 2 tablespoons lemon juice (or vinegar)
2 large handfuls fresh flat-leafed parsley

3 tablespoons fresh basil leaves, chopped
2 cloves garlic
1 anchovy (or 1 tablespoon Worcestershire sauce)
Coarse pepper to taste

Combine liquid ingredients and heat to boiling. Chop remaining ingredients by hand and add to hot sauce.

Or combine all ingredients in blender or food processor and chop coarsely with on-off pulse setting.

Pour over hot drained pasta and toss together.

Serves 4
Each portion (¼ of the recipe) provides a small fraction of your protein requirements.
With 2oz/50g cooked pasta, add: 1 ST

Baste à la Grecque

6 or 8 tablespoons plain low-fat yogurt
Juice of 1 lemon
3 tablespoons chopped fresh (or 1 tablespoon dried) mint

2 teaspoons fresh (or ½ teaspoon dried) oregano
Pinch each grated nutmeg and cinnamon
Salt (or garlic salt) and pepper, to taste

Fold ingredients together. Spread over lean lamb steaks, hamburger, chicken or fish. Refrigerate until cooking time. Grill or barbecue as desired.

Makes 6 portions
Each portion (2 tablespoons) provides a small fraction of your protein allowance.

Chinese Barbecue Sauce

6fl oz/175ml soy sauce
2 to 3 packets low-calorie sweetener

1 tablespoon grated orange rind
1 clove of garlic, crushed
Pepper to taste

Mix ingredients. Marinate any meat you wish for 1 hour or overnight. Prepare as desired.

Makes about 6fl oz/175ml
Nutrients provided by this sauce are negligible.

Marinade for Meat or Poultry

1½ teaspoons dry mustard
¾ teaspoon ground ginger
Pepper to taste

⅛ teaspoon garlic powder
6 tablespoons soy sauce
3 tablespoons lemon juice

Mix ingredients well. Marinate for 1 hour or overnight. Prepare meat as desired.

Makes about 4fl oz/100ml
Nutrients provided by this marinade are negligible.

Tangy Marinade

8 tablespoons plain low-fat yogurt
1 tablespoon each prepared
mustard, Worcestershire sauce,
and lemon juice
1 clove garlic, crushed

1 teaspoon dried herbs (thyme,
oregano, savory, rosemary, etc.)
Salt (or seasoned salt) and coarse
black pepper, to taste

Combine ingredients and spread over lean beef steaks, beef skirt or cut-up frying chicken pieces. Cover and marinate 30 minutes at room temperature or several hours in the refrigerator. Leaving the mixture on the food, grill or barbecue until done.

Serves 2
Each portion (½ of the recipe) provides: ⅓ ML

Spicy Cajun Marinade

6fl oz/175ml spicy tomato juice
3 tablespoons each
Worcestershire sauce and lemon
juice

2 cloves garlic, crushed
½ teaspoon (dried) thyme
Optional: 1 to 2 teaspoons chilli
sauce

Combine ingredients. Marinate meat or poultry for about 30 minutes at room temperature, or for several hours in the refrigerator. Marinate fish for a shorter period, depending upon type and thickness.

Makes about 8fl oz/225ml
Nutrients provided by this marinade are negligible.

Hawaiian Marinade

4fl oz/100ml each white wine,
unsweetened pineapple juice
3 tablespoons soy sauce

2 cloves garlic, crushed
1 tablespoon ground ginger

Combine ingredients. Pour over meat or poultry and refrigerate several hours. If meat is frozen, put it in a plastic bag and add marinating liquid. Let meat defrost in mixture.

Makes about 12fl oz/350ml
Nutrients provided by this marinade are negligible.

NINETEEN

Snacks, Drinks and Desserts

Yogurt Cheese

Drip-type coffee cone and filter paper

Optional: pinch of salt
1lb/450g plain low-fat yogurt

Line a coffee cone with filter paper and arrange it over a coffee pot. If you are using salt, gently mix into the yogurt. Empty the yogurt into the lined coffee cone. Put everything in the refrigerator and allow the yogurt to drain 6 to 8 hours until reduced by half (more or less, for a firmer or softer cheese).

Cheese may be wrapped in the filter paper. The drained liquid is known as 'whey' and is very nutritious though low in calories; save it to add to soups or stews.

Makes about 8oz/225g
Each portion (2½ tablespoons) provides: 1 PR

Variation

Pimiento and Olive Cheese

8oz/225g Yogurt Cheese made without added salt
2oz/50g stuffed Spanish-style green olives, chopped

1 tablespoon olive brine (from jar of olives)

Mix ingredients lightly. Spoon into a crock, cover and store in the refrigerator.

Makes 1¼ cups
Each portion (2½ tablespoons) provides: 1 PR

Hungarian Chive Cheese

This recipe is a bit like Liptauer cheese, without the excess calories — and without the anchovies.

8oz/225g Yogurt Cheese (see page 184)
2 teaspoons each chives (or onions),
caraway seeds, drained capers,
chopped, and prepared mustard
Paprika

Gently mix Yogurt Cheese with remaining ingredients, except paprika. Shape into a mound and cover all over with paprika. Serve with crackers or use strips of green or red pepper as scoops.

Makes about 8oz/225g
Each portion (2¼ tablespoons) provides: 1 PR

Iced Coffee, Jamaican-Style

4 cups fresh strong coffee
2 teaspoons rum flavouring
Dash of ground allspice

Combine coffee, rum flavouring and allspice; chill. Pour over ice cubes in 4 tall glasses.

Serves 4
Nutrients provided by this beverage are negligible.

Light Wine Cooler

Dry red or white wine
Sugar-free or diet fizzy lemon or lime, or fizzy mineral water

Put ¼ pint/150ml red or white wine in a tall glass over ice; fill with fizzy drink and stir.

Serves 1
Limit to one serving a day as the allowance for alcoholic beverage.

Zesty Tomato Cooler

6fl oz/175ml tomato juice
1 tablespoon lemon juice

Dash each Worcestershire and hot
pepper sauce
Optional: 1 celery stalk

Combine juices and flavourings; pour ice cubes in a tall glass.
Use celery stalk as stirrer, if desired.

Serves 1
Each portion (1 cooler) provides: 1 VEG

3-Juice Fruit Punch

6fl oz/175ml each unsweetened
orange, grape and pineapple
frozen juice concentrates

4½ pints/1.75 litres soda water
Optional: fresh fruit for garnish

Allow fruit juice concentrates to thaw; combine with soda water
over a block of ice in a large punch bowl. Garnish with fresh
fruit, if desired.

For single servings Combine the thawed juice concentrates in a
pitcher and store in the refrigerator. To make one drink, pour 2
or 3 tablespoons of the 'syrup' over ice in a tall glass, then fill to
the top with sparkling water.

Makes 14 servings
Each portion (6fl oz/175ml) provides: 1 FR

Juicy Cooler

Frozen orange-juice concentrate
Bottled white grape juice

Brandy flavouring
Soda water

Combine 2 tablespoons orange-juice concentrate, 4 tablespoons
white grape juice, and a few drops of brandy flavouring with
soda water in a tall glass over ice. Store the thawed, undiluted
orange-juice concentrate and bottled grape juice in the
refrigerator.

Serves 1

Variation

Use red grape juice with rum flavouring.

Each portion (1 cooler) provides: 1 FR

Chomocha Milkshake

1 tablespoon plain cocoa
1 teaspoon instant coffee
4fl oz/100ml boiling water
4 to 6 ice cubes

5 tablespoons dry skimmed milk
powder
1 or 2 packets low-calorie
sweetener
Few drops vanilla extract

Combine cocoa, coffee and boiling water in blender; cover and process until dissolved. Add the ice cubes to the blender along with the remaining ingredients and process until ice is completely dissolved and shake is thick and frothy. Fills a large glass.

Serves 1
Each portion (1 milkshake) provides: 1 ML

Mousse Napoleon

2 sachets plain gelatin
4 tablespoons cold water
8fl oz/225ml hot coffee
2 teaspoons brandy flavouring

1lb/450g semi-skimmed ricotta
cheese
8fl oz/225ml fresh skimmed milk
1 packet (4-serving) vanilla instant
pudding mix
1 tablespoon plain cocoa powder

Combine gelatin and cold water in blender or food processor. Wait 1 minute for gelatin to soften. Meanwhile, combine coffee and brandy flavouring; heat to boiling. Add to blender; cover and process until all gelatin granules are dissolved. Add ricotta and process until completely smooth and non-grainy. Add milk and pudding mix; process until consistency is smooth. Spoon most of the mixture into shallow bowl reserving 8 tablespoonsful. Combine the reserved mixture with cocoa and mix well. Spoon the cocoa mixture in stripes on top of the dessert. Then use the tip of a knife to draw through the stripes in the opposite direction, making a feathery pattern. Or for a marbled mousse, simply drizzle the chocolate mixture into the dessert and swirl lightly (don't overmix). Chill several hours until set.

Serves 4
Each portion (¼ of the recipe) provides: 1 PR, ½ ST, ½ ML

No-Cook Chocolate Mousse

1 large egg	1 teaspoon instant coffee
1 sachet plain gelatin	4oz/100g low-fat cottage cheese
1 tablespoon cornflour	4fl oz/100ml cold, low-fat milk
1 tablespoon cold water	2½ tablespoons plain cocoa
8fl oz/225ml boiling water	9 packets low-calorie sweetener

Combine egg, gelatin, cornflour and cold water in a blender container. Blend just until gelatin and cornflour are moist. Wait 1 minute for gelatin granules to soften, then add boiling water. Cover and blend.

Add remaining ingredients, except the sweetener. Blend until mixture is completely smooth and free of granules. Add the sweetener and blend again. Pour into four dessert dishes and let set.

Serves 4
Each portion (¼ of the recipe) provides: 1 PR

Fruit Mousse Medley

1×6fl oz/175ml can orange-juice concentrate	6oz/175g semi-skimmed ricotta cheese
2 eggs, separated	Optional: low-calorie sweetener to equal 10 teaspoons (5 packets)
1×8oz/225g can juice-packed pineapple rings	Pinch of salt
Water	1 eating orange, peeled, cut in wedges
1 sachet plain gelatin	1 banana, sliced

Thaw orange juice concentrate but don't dilute. Separate eggs; put whites in an electric mixer bowl and yolks in blender or food processor.

Drain pineapple and reserve juice. Add enough water to pineapple juice to make 4fl oz/100ml; combine in a saucepan with gelatin. Wait 1 minute, then heat gently until gelatin melts. Remove from heat.

Beat egg yolks in food processor or blender, then add pineapple juice-gelatin mixture through the small opening while motor runs. Add undiluted orange juice concentrate, ricotta and low-calorie sweetener, if desired. Cover and process until completely smooth and blended. Chill until partly set.

Add a pinch of salt to egg whites and beat until stiff peaks form. Gently but thoroughly fold partly set gelatin mixture into beaten egg whites.

Arrange pineapple rings, orange wedges and banana slices vertically inside a glass serving dish; press lightly to the sides.

Spoon in gelatin mixture. Chill in refrigerator until set.

Serves 8
Each portion (⅛ of the recipe) provides: ⅛ PR, 1½ FR

Orange Cheese Mousse

4 tablespoons orange juice
8fl oz/225ml boiling water
1 tablespoon plain gelatin
12oz/350g cottage cheese

4 single-serving packets sugar-
  free vanilla milkshake mix
Optional: 8oz/225g fresh
  strawberries, sliced

Heat 2 tablespoons juice with water until boiling. Meanwhile, combine remaining 2 tablespoons juice with gelatin in blender or food processor. Allow gelatin to soften 1 minute. Add boiling water mixture to gelatin. Process until gelatin granules are dissolved; use a rubber scraper on the side of the container and process again. Add cottage cheese and process until completely smooth and creamy. Add vanilla mix and process completely smooth.

Chill until set. Arrange sliced strawberries (or other fresh fruit) on top of mousse before serving, if desired.

Serves 10

Variation

Orange Chocolate Cheese Mousse

Substitute sugar-free chocolate milkshake mix for the vanilla mix. Top with fresh orange slices, if desired.

Each portion (¹/₁₀ of the recipe) provides: ⅓ PR, ⅓ ML
With fruit add: ½ FR

Lime Mousse

2 eggs
1 sachet plain gelatin
8fl oz/225ml boiling water
4fl oz/100ml fresh lime juice

6 ice cubes
5 packets sugar-free vanilla
milkshake mix

Beat eggs and gelatin together. Wait 1 minute until gelatin softens, then beat in boiling water, until gelatin granules melt. Add lime juice. Beat in ice cubes, one at a time. Beat in milkshake mix. Spoon into dessert dishes and chill until set.

Serves 6
Each portion (¹/₆ of the recipe) provides: ¾ ML

Peach Cheesecake

1 sachet plain gelatin
6fl oz/175ml unsweetened peach
nectar (or other fruit juice)
8oz/225g low-fat cream cheese
8oz/225g cottage cheese

Optional: 6 packets low-calorie
sweetener
4 large digestive biscuits broken
up
1½ cups fresh sliced peaches (or
apricots)

Coat a non-stick square cake tin generously with cooking oil. Combine gelatin and 2 tablespoons peach nectar in blender or food processor. While gelatin softens, heat remaining peach nectar to boiling. Add hot nectar to gelatin mixture; cover and process until gelatin granules are completely dissolved. Add cream cheese, cottage cheese and sweetener, if used; process until completely smooth. Arrange digestive biscuits in the bottom of the cake pan. Spoon cheese mixture over biscuits and chill until set. Just before serving, peel and slice peaches (coat peach slices with lemon juice and sweetener to taste, if desired) and arrange slices on top of cheese filling. Cut into squares to serve.

Serves 12
Each portion ($^1/_{12}$ of the recipe) provides: 1 PR, $^1/_6$ ST, $^1/_4$ FR

Fruited Cheesecake

4 eggs, separated
12oz/350g low-fat cottage cheese
4 tablespoons plain or vanilla low-fat yogurt

7 to 9 packets low-calorie sweetener, divided
12oz/350g sliced fresh strawberries, or a mixture of fresh fruit
2 tablespoons lemon juice

Separate egg yolks into a blender and egg whites into a mixing bowl. Add cheese and yogurt to the egg yolks. Cover and blend until smooth.

Beat egg whites stiff with electric mixer. Pour egg yolk-cheese mixture into egg whites and gently, but thoroughly, fold together (don't overmix).

Grease an 8- or 9-in/20 or 22.5cm springform pan, then spoon batter into it. Bake in a preheated 350°F/180°C/Mark 4 oven for approximately 45 minutes, until puffy. Remove cake from the oven and let it set for 10 minutes. Sprinkle with three packets of sweetener. When cool, chill in refrigerator.

While cake is chilling, stir the fruit together with the lemon juice and the remaining sweetener. Refrigerate until serving time. Spoon fruit on to the cheesecake just before serving. (*Note:* canned fruit, drained, may be used instead of fresh fruit.)

Serves 6
Each portion ($^1/_6$ of the recipe) provides: 1 PR, 1 FR

Crustless Cherry Cheese Pie

1 sachet plain gelatin
1 egg
4 tablespoons apple juice
6fl oz/175ml boiling water

12oz/350g low-fat cottage cheese
8 packets low-calorie sweetener
4oz/100g fresh cherries

Combine gelatin and egg in blender or food processor; process until mixed. Combine juice and water; heat to boiling. With machine running, add hot liquid through the opening in top. Process until gelatin granules are dissolved. Stop machine and scrape down the container sides with a rubber scraper, then process again. Add cottage cheese and sweetener; process until cheese is smooth. Chill until mixture begins to set.

Meanwhile, cut cherries in half and remove stones. Fold gently into cheese mixture, then spoon filling into a glass pie dish.

Serves 10
Each portion (¹/₁₀ of the recipe) provides: 1 PR, ½ FR

Apricot Cheese Pie

1 tablespoon diet margarine
2oz/50g digestive biscuit crumbs
1lb/450g low-fat cottage cheese
4 tablespoons apricot nectar
3 eggs

Pinch of salt
2½oz/60g each sultanas and dried apricots, finely chopped
Ground cinnamon

Spread margarine over bottom of a non-stick 8-in/20-cm pie dish. Sprinkle on biscuit crumbs; press firmly over bottom of pan.

Combine cheese, nectar, eggs and salt in blender or food processor container. Process smooth, scraping down sides of container with rubber scraper. Pour half of this filling mixture into pie dish. Sprinkle sultanas and apricots evenly over filling. Pour on remaining filling covering all fruit. Sprinkle with cinnamon.

Bake in preheated 325°F/170°C/Mark 3 oven 45 to 55 minutes, or until filling is set. Cool before serving.

Serves 8
Each portion (⅛ of the pie) provides: 1 PR, ½ ST, 1 FR

Black and White Pie

8fl oz/225ml low-fat milk	8 packets low-calorie sweetener
1 sachet plain gelatin	4 tablespoons plain cocoa powder
6oz/175g low-fat cottage cheese	2 egg whites
2 teaspoons vanilla extract or rum flavouring	Pinch of salt

Put half of the milk into a saucepan. Sprinkle the gelatin over it. Soften 1 minute, then heat gently, stirring until the gelatin is completely dissolved.

Place cottage cheese in blender. Cover and blend until completely smooth. Add gelatin mixture, remaining milk and vanilla. Cover and blend until smooth. Put half of the blended mixture into a mixing bowl and set it aside.

To the half of the mixture remaining in the blender, add 4 packets sweetener and cocoa. Blend thoroughly. Pour into a greased 8-inch/20-cm pie dish and chill until partially set – about 30 minutes.

Beat egg whites and salt until stiff. Gradually beat in the remaining sweetener. Gently but thoroughly fold into the vanilla half of the mixture. Spoon over chocolate layer and chill several hours until completely set.

Serves 6
Each portion (¹⁄₆ of the pie) provides: 1 PR

Crustless Chocolate Cinnamon Pie

8fl oz/225ml cold skimmed milk	1 packet (4-serving) sugar-free
1 sachet plain gelatin	instant chocolate pudding mix
6fl oz/175ml boiling water	1 teaspoon vanilla extract
4 or 5 ice cubes	½ teaspoon ground cinnamon
8oz/225g low-fat cottage cheese	Optional: 2 or 3 packets low-calorie sweetener

Put 3 or 4 tablespoons of milk in the bottom of food processor or blender container and sprinkle with gelatin. Wait 1 minute until gelatin is soft, then add boiling water. Process until gelatin is completely dissolved (scrape sides of container with rubber scraper). Add ice cubes; process until melted. Add cottage cheese; process until completely smooth and creamy. Add remaining ingredients; process smooth (add sweetener to taste last, if desired). Spoon the mixture into a glass pie dish.

Serves 8
Each portion (⅛ of the recipe) provides: ½ PR, ½ ST, ⅛ ML

Crustless Chomocha Pie

1 sachet plain gelatin
6 tablespoons water
2 teaspoons instant coffee powder
8fl oz/225ml fresh skimmed milk

8oz/225g semi-skimmed ricotta cheese
4-serving packet sugar-free instant chocolate pudding mix

Sprinkle gelatin on water. Wait 1 minute, then heat gently, until gelatin dissolves. Remove from heat and stir in instant coffee until dissolved.

In food processor or blender, combine milk and ricotta; process completely smooth. Add gelatin mixture; process smooth. Add pudding mix; process until smooth. Chill several hours in glass pie dish and keep refrigerated. (Leftover pie can be sliced into single-serving wedges and frozen. Thaw several hours in the refrigerator before serving.)

Serves 8
Each portion (⅛ of the recipe) provides: ½ PR, ½ ST

Poached Pears with Raspberry Sauce

This recipe comes from Adrian's Café in Philadelphia.

3¼ pints/2 litres water
Half lemon, sliced
1 cinnamon stick
6 firm fresh pears

6 to 8oz/175 to 225g frozen unsweetened raspberries
Low-calorie sweetener
Optional: fresh mint leaves

Fill a pot with cold water and add lemon slices and cinnamon stick.

Peel the pears, leaving the stem and a little cap of skin near the stem. Place each pear in the cold water as soon as it's peeled. Simmer just until cooked through but not mushy, about 6 to 8 minutes. Drain pears on paper towels, then chill thoroughly in the refrigerator. Split each pear in half and remove the core with a tablespoon.

To make sauce, thaw the raspberries and purée them smooth in the blender or food processor, sweetening to taste. Arrange each cored pear half on top of its sauce. Garnish with some fresh mint, if desired.

Serves 12
Each portion (¹/₁₂ of the recipe) provides: 1½ FR

Blueberry Jel-Low

1 sachet plain gelatin
8fl oz/225ml each cold water,
chilled bottled unsweetened grape juice

6 packets low-calorie sweetener, or to taste
8oz/225g fresh blueberries

Sprinkle gelatin on half the water in a small saucepan. Wait 1 minute, then heat gently until melted. Remove from heat and stir in remaining water, grape juice and sweetener. Refrigerate until syrupy, then fold in berries. Chill until set.

Serves 4
Each portion (¼ of the recipe) provides: 1 FR

Luscious Lime Parfait

1 sachet unflavoured gelatin
4 tablespoons cold water
8fl oz/225ml boiling water
4oz/100g low-fat cottage cheese

5 tablespoons lime juice
3 egg whites
Pinch of salt
8 packets low-calorie sweetener

Sprinkle gelatin over cold water in blender. Wait 1 minute for gelatin to soften, then add boiling water. Blend until gelatin is dissolved. Add cottage cheese and blend until smooth. Add lime juice and blend. Refrigerate until partially set.

Beat egg whites and salt until soft peaks form. Beat in sweetener.

Beat partially set gelatin mixture until light and fluffy. Gently fold into beaten egg whites. Spoon into 10 parfait glasses. Top each with a sprinkle of grated peel or a few digestive biscuit crumbs, if desired.

Serves 10
Each portion (¹/₁₀ of the recipe) provides: ½ PR

Frozen Bananas

Bananas are easy to freeze and have lots of uses in the low-cal sugar-free kitchen: in drinks, for ice-cream and frozen yogurts, in parfaits.

Simply peel and slice them thick or thin. Spread the slices in a single layer, touching, on a sheet of plastic or foil and cover tightly to keep out the air. Label and freeze, then take out only what you need.

The best bananas for freezing are the ripest, skins generously freckled. The riper they are, the more natural sweetness. Storing banana slices in the freezer for later use is a very good way to use up over-ripe bananas that have lots of flavour but are too mushy for out-of-hand eating. However, for best colour, taste and texture, frozen bananas should be used fairly soon, within a few weeks if possible. If you plan to freeze them longer, squirt some lemon juice over the slices before you wrap and freeze them. Lemon adds delicious tang to these recipes; you might like the lemon-kissed version better.

Banana 'Ice-Cream'

3 small (or 2 large) ripe bananas, peeled, sliced and frozen

6 to 7 tablespoons fresh skimmed milk

Put the frozen banana slices in your food processor (using the steel blade) or in a blender. Process until frozen bananas are chopped and grainy but still frozen. Add the milk a few tablespoons at a time and process until smooth and creamy, the texture of frozen custard. Serve immediately. Don't add too much milk or process too long or mixture will become too soft.

With an electric mixer If you don't have a food processor or blender, you can make Banana 'Ice-Cream' with an electric mixer. However, it won't be as quick and convenient. Here's how: don't freeze the bananas. Peel them and combine them with the milk in an electric mixer bowl, then beat them smooth. Spoon the mixture into ice cube trays and freeze firm. Remove banana cubes from freezer and put them in the electric mixer bowl. Let soften slightly several minutes, then quickly beat the cubes into a fluffy frost that resembles frozen custard. Serve immediately.

If you have an ice-cream maker, beat the fresh banana and milk together, then spoon the mixture into the appliance and process according to manufacturer's directions.

Variations

Frozen Banana Yogurt

Substitute plain low-fat yogurt for the milk.

Serves 4
Each portion (¼ of the recipe) provides: 1 FR, ⅛ ML

Orange Banana Sherbert

Substitute orange juice for the milk.

Provides 1⅛ FR

Other Variations

Sweeten to taste, if desired, with 1 or 2 packets low-calorie sweetener. Make a tangy banana-buttermilk sorbet by using buttermilk instead of milk. Use other fruit juices: pineapple, apple or apricot, or try grape for a frozen Banana Blush. Vary the flavour with a few drops of brandy or rum flavouring, or use 2 tablespoons rum and 4 or 5 tablespoons water instead of milk.

Flavour with vanilla or coconut extract, if desired.

Banana Strawberry Sundae

Better than a banana split!

Banana 'Ice-Cream' (see page 196)
4oz/100g fresh (or thawed) unsweetened strawberries

Make Banana 'Ice-Cream' as directed and spoon into three stemmed goblets or sundae dishes. Store the desserts briefly in the freezer while you prepare the sauce.

Rinse, but do not wash, food processor or blender. Put the washed hulled strawberries (or thawed strawberries) into the unit and process until chopped or puréed into a bright red sauce (sweeten, if desired, with a few packets low-calorie sweetener). Drizzle the sauce over the ice-cream.

Serves 4
Each portion (¼ of the recipe) provides: 1¼ FR, ⅛ ML

Bananectarina 'Ice-Cream'

2 bananas, peeled, sliced thin, and frozen (see page 196)

1 large unpeeled nectarine (or 2 small unpeeled peaches, sliced)
2 tablespoons ice-cold water

Slice the bananas thin and freeze. At dessert time, dice the nectarine (no need to peel, the flecks of peel add colour, flavour and fibre). Combine ingredients in food processor and process smooth, adding another tablespoon or two of water, if needed.

Serves 5
Each portion (⅕ of the recipe) provides: 1 FR

Berry Banana 'Ice-Cream'

This recipe is high in fibre

4oz/100g raspberries (or blackberries)
3 or 4 tablespoons water

2 bananas, peeled, sliced thin, and frozen (see page 196)

Rinse raspberries and reserve some for garnish. Combine remaining raspberries and frozen banana slices in food processor; process to the texture of soft ice-cream, adding water a tablespoon at a time. (If you are not milk-intolerant, you could substitute skimmed milk for the water.) Serve immediately, garnished with a few fresh berries. (For a sweeter dessert add low-calorie sweetener to taste.)

Variation

Banana Strawberry 'Ice-Cream'

Substitute sliced fresh strawberries for the raspberries.

Serves 6
Each portion ($\frac{1}{6}$ of the recipe) provides: 1 FR

Banana Pineapple Sundae

2 bananas, peeled, sliced thin, and frozen (see page 196)
2 to 4 tablespoons unsweetened pineapple juice

Few drops rum flavouring
4 tablespoons juice-packed crushed pineapple, drained

Combine frozen bananas with juice and rum flavouring in food processor. Process until the texture of soft ice-cream. Serve immediately in parfait glasses with crushed pineapple on top.

Serves 5
(Each portion ($\frac{1}{5}$ of the recipe) provides: 1 FR

Tricolor Banana Parfaits

2 ripe bananas, peeled, sliced thin, and frozen (see page 196)

4oz/100g each fresh blueberries and sliced strawberries

To assemble parfaits, arrange the banana slices between a layer of blueberries and a layer of strawberries in a tulip sundae bowl.

Serves 6
Each portion ($\frac{1}{6}$ of the recipe) provides: 1½ FR

Frozen Banana Milkshake

One of the best ways to use frozen banana slices is in frosty milkshakes. The banana chills the milk.

Several slices frozen banana (equal to half a banana) (see page 196)

6fl oz/175ml fresh skimmed milk
Few drops vanilla extract

Combine in blender and process smooth. Add a shake of cinnamon, if desired.

Serves 1
Each portion (1 shake) provides: ¾ ML, 1 FR

Index

Index compiled by Peva Keane

Barbara Griggs
The Home Herbal: A Handbook of Simple Remedies £3.99

When it was first published, this book was hailed as an informative and authoritative guide to simple herbal remedies for home use. Now completely revised and updated, it is even more valuable and deserves a place on every family bookshelf.

The Home Herbal makes no claims for miracle cures. But it does offer a sensible and systematic guide to herbal remedies for a whole range of ailments where conventional medicine can often fail to provide relief or produces unpleasant side-effects, and for those minor medical problems such as sunburn, coughs and colds and hangovers which can benefit from natural, gentle treatment by herbs.

The book is organised alphabetically under medical problems, from acne through depression and insomnia to whooping cough, and herbal remedies are suggested under each of these headings. In addition there are chapters on the preparation of herbal medicines, where to find your herbs and how to stock your family medicine cupboard. A new feature of this edition is the section devoted to children's ailments.

Elizabeth Taylor
Elizabeth Takes Off £3.99

At some point in their lives, almost everyone suffers the pangs of notching up a few unwanted pounds. But for Elizabeth Taylor, the world's media were standing by to record her downfall as she gave in to an addiction just as compulsive as drink or drugs.

With compelling candour, she tells of the private anguish that led her to seek solace in food – and the bitter realisation before her bedroom mirror that enough was enough. Included too, is the diet and exercise regime that helped her look – not as good as before – but even better!

In an age where slimness is an international obsession, her story is "a victory for anyone who has ever lost their self-image and self-esteem" – and an inspiration to anyone who wants to win them back.

'Elizabeth Taylor's is the first superstar health and beauty book I have read that convinces me that the writer really has been through the mill'
DAILY TELEGRAPH

'The most eagerly awaited book for years'. *DAILY EXPRESS*

'This book is not just to set the record straight about why I gained weight and how I lost it . . . and it's more than a specific programme for weight loss: It's a chance for you to throw away old self-destructive habits and embrace a positive way of life'. ELIZABETH TAYOR

All Pan books are available at your local bookshop or newsagent, or can be ordered direct from the publisher. Indicate the number of copies required and fill in the form below.

Send to: **CS Department, Pan Books Ltd., P.O. Box 40, Basingstoke, Hants.   RG21 2YT.**

or phone: 0256 469551 (Ansaphone), quoting title, author and Credit Card number.

Please enclose a remittance* to the value of the cover price plus: 60p for the first book plus 30p per copy for each additional book ordered to a maximum charge of £2.40 to cover postage and packing.

*Payment may be made in sterling by UK personal cheque, postal order, sterling draft or international money order, made payable to Pan Books Ltd.

Alternatively by Barclaycard/Access:

Card No. | | | | | | | | | | | | | | | | | |

Signature:

Applicable only in the UK and Republic of Ireland.

While every effort is made to keep prices low, it is sometimes necessary to increase prices at short notice. Pan Books reserve the right to show on covers and charge new retail prices which may differ from those advertised in the text or elsewhere.

NAME AND ADDRESS IN BLOCK LETTERS PLEASE:

....

Name————————————————————————————

Address————————————————————————————

————————————————————————————

————————————————————————————

————————————————————————————

3/87